NEOCONOMY

NEOCONOMY

George Bush's Revolutionary Gamble with America's Future

DANIEL ALTMAN

PublicAffairs

New York

Book design by Mark McGarry
Set in Meridien

Library of Congress Cataloging-in-Publication data
Neoconomy : George Bush's revolutionary gamble with America's future
/ Daniel Altman.
p. cm.   Includes bibliographical references and index.
ISBN 1-58648-229-7
1. United States—Economic policy—2001- 2. United States—Economic
conditions—2001- 3. Council of Economic Advisers (U.S.) 4. Bush,
George W. (George Walker), 1946– 5. Elite (Social science)—United
States. 6. Economic forecasting—United States. I. Title: George Bush's
revolutionary gamble with America's future. II. Title.
HC106.83.A45 2004
330.973—dc22
2004050398

FIRST EDITION
10 9 8 7 6 5 4 3 2 1

To Katherine and Sebastian, who made me do this

CONTENTS

PART III

ACKNOWLEDGMENTS

This being my first book, I have lots of people to thank. At the top of the list are my parents, who have made everything possible. Everyone should be lucky enough to have such enthusiastic, patient and trusting backers.

I've already expressed my appreciation for my academic mentors in the acknowledgments to my doctoral dissertation, so I won't take up much more space here. I only want to say that I hope I've made good use of the tools they taught, despite—or perhaps because of—doing so outside the ivory tower. I especially hope that Martin S. Feldstein, my longtime adviser, won't take umbrage at any of my passages concerning his work. We haven't always seen eye-to-eye on the political economy of the United States, but my respect for him and debt to him are both profound.

For the past few years, I've made a practice of telling

the odd aspiring journalist how fortunate I was that the editors at *The Economist* decided to take a chance on me. They hired a writer with almost no professional experience, and I learned a huge amount about real-world economics from them. They possess the intuitive, rather than academic, economic sensibility that I have often tried to transmit in this book.

The same goes for many of my former colleagues at *The New York Times*, who also offered me opportunities I never would have expected. Without the skills and personal visibility I gained there, this book would never have appeared. The article that was its precursor, "The End of Taxes As We Know Them," appeared in the *Times* on March 30, 2003. I'm also grateful for the editors' forbearance following my decision to leave the *Times* and start this manuscript.

Robert Preskill, my agent, championed this project with an unbeatable combination of energy and savvy from the moment I emailed him the idea. He deserves many more clients with more lucrative prospects than mine. Thanks go to him, and also to Mildred Marmur for introducing the two of us. And more thanks are due to Peter Osnos and Clive Priddle at PublicAffairs, who shared Rob's confidence in me and my ideas, and to the super sales and marketing team at PublicAffairs and Perseus.

As any reader of the endnotes in this book will quickly discern, the statistical wings of the United States government played an enormous part in its writing. They deserve extraordinary credit for putting an ocean of data, press materials and legislative documents online in user-friendly formats. The easy accessibility of so much information about the government's actions and the behavior of the economy is a great boon, both for science and for democracy.

Like any reporter, I'm especially grateful to everyone who ever returned one of my calls. Special help with figures on unemployment benefits came from Maurice Emsellem and Andrew Stettner of the National Employment Law Project. Robert S. McIntyre, director of Citizens for Tax Justice, provided estimates of tax and income distributions from his group's computer model. David I. Laibson, who was one of my professors at Harvard, supplied a sheaf of useful material on American overoptimism. Thanks to all of them for their patience and generosity with their time.

Though I enjoyed writing this book, I am grateful to my friends, as well as to my sister and her family, for keeping me sane during those heady five months. There's nothing like driving a four-wheeler through the Scottish countryside to take your mind off labor market statistics.

Along the way, I received valuable advice from a bevy of book-writing buddies, including Alex Berenson, David Cay Johnston and Barry Meier from the *Times* and my compatriot from *The Economist*, Vijay Vaitheeswaran. May they all sell more copies than I do.

A few people did me the huge favor of reading the text before publication. To them I owe many delicious dinners, nights of babysitting and days of reciprocal editing. Francisco Perez-Gonzalez, my comrade, knows economics better than I do and is a nicer guy, to boot. Another reader who preferred, understandably, to remain anonymous is probably the smartest guy I know, and I know a lot of smart guys (he's nice, too). Sebastian Conley has been my most steadfast friend for a dozen years. Yes, it's hard to believe anyone could last that long. And Katherine Zoepf, who will always be a better writing stylist and a better person than me, is my own personal ray of sunlight.

All errors and omissions, if not transposed directly from governmental or otherwise theoretically reliable sources, are my own responsibility. There are a lot of better writers and better economists out there. I hope some of them will join me in taking on this topic.

INTRODUCTION

O God, that one might read the book of fate
And see the revolution of the times.

—WILLIAM SHAKESPEARE

A revolution is brewing in Washington, and it has nothing to do with the foreign policy that has seen America
send troops to Afghanistan, Iraq, Jordan and the Philip-
pines. While the neoconservatives in the State Department, the Defense Department and the National
Security Agency line up more targets along the Axis of
Evil, another cadre of neocons is well on its way to
transforming American society. They have been at work
since the beginning of George W. Bush's term, putting
their plans in place one piece at a time. They have
stayed out of the limelight, even seeking to camouflage
their agenda. They are the neoconomists, and their goal
is the neoconomy.

Unlike the upheaval in foreign policy, the neoconomists' revolution is certainly not being televised. There
was no big speech by President Bush to mark its birth,

no catchphrase ready-made for the headlines. The rationale for its radical agenda can be found in academic papers, not Congressional testimony. Yet through every major event of the Bush presidency, the administration's focus on the neoconomy has remained acute. And though many people may not even realize that a revolution is afoot, it could change their lives dramatically—for better, or for worse.

It's time to start paying attention, both for Americans and for the rest of the world. The economy of the United States makes up a third of the entire world's output of goods and services, and it accounts for more than a sixth of all the world's trade. When it booms, the rest of the world usually booms with it. When it busts, the repercussions are felt almost everywhere.

The neoconomists' revolution has one goal: to increase the rate at which the economy grows by changing how the nation uses its resources. It is a worthy goal, too. An increase of just 0.1 percent in the rate of economic growth, which usually averages around 3 percent a year, would enlarge the nation's annual income by $10 billion. That's enough to pay to roughly the entire population of Cincinnati the nation's median annual income. Or to take every single American out for a steak dinner. Or to give a reasonable education to all of the roughly 1.5 million elementary and high school students in North Carolina for a year. Or to buy seven B–2 Spirit "stealth" bombers.

Every year, the federal government spends about 200 of those $10 billion chunks. But as George W. Bush has realized, the savvy politician can lay his hands on many more. By committing the nation to policies that could last a decade into the future, or longer, he has made sure that several trillion dollars more are already spoken for.

Making big changes in a big economy implies big risks. Following the path chosen by the neoconomists could indeed lead to a period of untold prosperity, with living standards rising faster than ever before. It could also lead to nothing less than the collapse of the capitalist system—a real revolution in which the nation's taxpaying laborers rise up against a class of wealthy free-riders.

This is not sensationalism. These possibilities do not follow from moral judgments or political ideologies. They are the result of economic logic. That logic has propelled the neoconomists in their quest to remake America. It could also become their undoing.

PART 1

1

THE SETTING

Industrial man—a sentient reciprocating engine
having a fluctuating output, coupled to an iron
wheel revolving with uniform velocity. And then
we wonder why this should be the golden age of
revolution . . .

—ALDOUS HUXLEY

At the turn of the millennium, the economy was leaving
behind a period of rising expectations and entering a
period of general uncertainty. From the viewpoint of
many economists, the boom of the 1990's had been a
long hoped-for payoff after decades of rapid technological advancement. There was no doubt about what had
driven the economy through the 1990's; the engine was
clear. But no one knew what would come next. Long-
running trends and unexpected events would affect not
only how much the Bush administration's policies might
help the economy, but also how much the nation could
afford them.

Even this uncertainty, however, could not dampen
the good news that arrived in January 2001, just after
George W. Bush took office. In the coming decade, the
federal government was poised to rack up $5.6 trillion

in budget surpluses. This forecast came from the Congressional Budget Office. After rolling together its predictions about the economy, the office concluded that the Treasury would collect $5.6 trillion more in taxes between 2002 and 2011 than the government would spend.

The actual size of those surpluses, once they arrived, would depend in part on how well the economy really performed. It was far from easy to predict how much businesses would produce and consumers would spend in a year, let alone a decade. Any changes in Congress's taxing and spending plans would also change the forecast. And a stickler might argue that only the surpluses expected to arrive in budget years 2002 through 2005, amounting to a mere $1.5 trillion, were relevant to President Bush's term.

Still, the message was clear: the federal government would probably have some extra money to play with. These anticipated surpluses would almost definitely offer the new president some wiggle-room in a crisis. Given his father's woeful example—one term and out, thanks to the perception that he did nothing about the last recession—that cushion must have made George W. Bush smile.

Not surprisingly, President Bush's predecessor had already proposed a use for the money. In 1999, the Clinton administration outlined a plan to eliminate the huge debts the nation had accumulated through a half-century of mostly unbalanced budgets. The plan required the federal government to buy back the $3.6 trillion in

Treasury notes, bonds and bills held by the public at that time.* It would take ten years and would use a large portion of the budget surpluses, which had just begun to pile up. President Clinton also wanted to set some of the anticipated surpluses aside to help Social Security and Medicare deal with the challenge of an aging population. The first course of action would reduce the Treasury's indebtedness; the second would help the federal government to pay all the benefits it had promised to the baby boomers in their retirement.

The problem with President Clinton's plan was that most of those budget surpluses would not appear until years after he left office. He could not impose his will on his successors. And George W. Bush had other ideas.

Like his predecessor, President Bush had no qualms about speaking for all $5.6 trillion in surpluses, even though only $1.5 trillion were expected during his first term. But he decided to hold onto some of the money, at least at first, ensuring that his wiggle-room stayed in place. He called it a $1.4 trillion "contingency fund," though the contingency was unspoken. Another $1.6 trillion would fulfill his election-year promise to cut taxes; the enormous cuts would be spread out over ten years. The remaining $2.6 trillion belonged to the trust funds held by Social Security and other government programs, but Mr. Bush said he would use $2 trillion of that money to repay the nation's debt *outside* of those

---

* A couple more trillions in debt are held by the Federal Reserve Board and within the government's own accounts.

programs' own gigantic liabilities. He'd find another way, he said, to make sure they were solvent.

There was a big, important difference between the plans put forward by President Clinton and President Bush. The federal government could only pay off its debts if those anticipated surpluses actually appeared. If a hypothetical government had to spend $100 a year on its normal operations and collected exactly $100 in taxes, it couldn't pay off any debts without being forced to borrow more. Only if the government collected more than $100 in taxes, without raising spending, could it pay back any debt with no other consequences.

In this way, a plan for debt reduction would respond automatically to changes in the economy, taxes or spending. Whatever happened in the future, the government could never use money that it didn't have.

Yet after a tax cut became law, its effects would take hold regardless of the state of the government's balance sheet. Even if the government sank into deep deficits, pushing tax rates back up would require new legislation. As a result, a ten-year slate of tax cuts represented a far greater—and riskier—commitment than a ten-year program to pay off the nation's debt.

It may not have been obvious at the time, but George W. Bush's plan also included the first step on a path of peaceful revolution. Traveling that path would transform the American economy, and perhaps American society along with it. Back in early 2001, however, people were more worried about what the next year would hold.

*

To understand exactly where the economy stood, it is worth considering an earlier period of uncertainty. In the early 1990's, experts were puzzling over a recent slowdown in the growth of workers' productivity. Productivity is the amount of goods and services a worker can generate during a fixed period of time. It typically increases when companies buy more or better capital—software, equipment, machines, and the like—for their workers to use, or when workers figure out more intelligent ways to use that capital. Workers' productivity also rises when the underlying value or quality of the goods and services they generate increases.

For most of the 20th century, workers' productivity in the private sector had been improving by an average of about 2.2 percent a year. In the 1980's, however, that growth dropped off to just 1.5 percent, in what some economists called "The Great Productivity Slowdown." For several years, figuring out the causes of this lag was one of the most important, and puzzling, problems in economics.

Important, because gains in productivity were the surest route to higher standards of living. Making the average person better off, in a material sense, means generating more income for each person in the economy. There is a limited number of ways to do that: more people could join the labor force, the people in the labor force could work more hours, or the people in the labor force could become more productive. Since the share of people who work and the hours they work change only slightly from year to year—and do not always rise—

gains in productivity supply most of the nation's improvements in living standards.

Puzzling, because the nation had just experienced an explosion of innovation. Personal computers, data networks, mobile telephones, fast fiber optic telephone lines, compact discs—all of these technologies became viable, if not widely available, in the 1970's and early 1980's. How was it possible, given these advances, that workers were having trouble becoming more productive? Economists wondered whether the nation had too few well-educated workers to take advantage of the new tools. They also wondered whether the productivity gains of the past would ever return.

By the end of the 1990's, their questions—and prayers—had been answered. It took time for the information-based technologies to become inexpensive and user-friendly enough to be incorporated into the working habits of the general population. But once people were used to desktops, laptops, pagers and wireless phones, the economy leapt forward. Workers' productivity grew by almost 2.7 percent a year from 1996 through 2000, and the nation's median household income grew from $35,492 in 1996 to $41,990 in 2000.

With the sky apparently the limit for the wealth to be reaped from new technologies, companies made record-breaking investments in equipment and hired millions more workers. The economy expanded at a breakneck pace of 4 percent a year from 1996 to 2000. In April 2000, the unemployment rate dropped to 3.8 percent— a 30-year low.

It was a sort of slingshot effect: first you pulled back while you invested in new technologies, then, once they became assimilated into the economy, you sprang forward by reaping the gains from those investments. The frustrating adjustment period had paid off with a decade of broadband-fast growth. But a new question arose towards the end of the 1990's: was this a new kind of normal, or just another blip?

If it had been a blip, then the nation would eventually revert to earlier notions of normalcy: unemployment at 5 or 6 percent, economic growth of about 3 percent per year and productivity gains of about 2 percent annually. Getting there would be painful—it would feel like a recession, whether or not the economy actually shrank—but not much could be done about it, short of discovering a new engine.

To judge by the experience of the late 20th century, finding a new engine would not be easy. The advances of the 1970's had incubated for two decades before empowering the economy, and their development could not be chalked up to any one policy decision. Changing any fundamentals of the economy—education levels, management techniques, scientific knowledge, financial markets, laws and attitudes—took time.

For a government facing all these forms of uncertainty, choosing a successful, long-term economic policy would not be easy. If the future held more of the wonders of the 1990's, the federal budget surpluses would continue to pile up and the labor market would sop up workers like a sponge. Experimenting with different kinds of tax systems, government programs and budget rules would come at little long-term cost, since the economy would be operating with a substantial cushion.

If more humdrum times were on the way, however, a painful adjustment period would be inevitable. Any prodding by the government might have about as much effect on the economy as on a dead mule.

If the economy's long-term prospects were less than promising at the dawn of 2001, the short-term signs were downright threatening.

The ill omens started with the stock markets. According to research conducted in the 1980's and 1990's, America's stock markets have shown themselves to be a reasonable indicator of where the economy is heading. The reason is simple: the value of a stock depends primarily on the future profits of the company that issues it.

When the stock market crashed in the spring of 2000, it sent a signal that the huge expectations of the 1990's—namely, that fast-growing companies based on the Internet would soon take over all commerce, which would flow along the fiber optic lines laid by other fast-growing companies—would not be met anytime soon. The main index of the Nasdaq over-the-counter market, which included most of the businesses in that category that had gone public, fell by two-thirds in just 13 months.

Unfortunately, the effect snowballed. Some companies with high expectations had used their equally high stock prices to pad their profits. They would buy smaller, more profitable businesses using their stock—rarely would they pay much of the purchase price in cash—and then add those businesses' earnings to their own bottom lines. With share prices falling, this practice became harder to maintain.

Stock options became worthless, too, as share prices fell, dealing another blow to the nation's wealth. With less wealth, people's demand for goods and services fell. Slack demand for companies' products led to further falls in share prices, and more worthless options. The snowball got bigger.

Corporate profits took a dive in 2000, falling to $818 billion from $851 billion in 1999. It was bad news for the federal government, which relied on taxes on corporate profits for about 20 percent of the revenue it collected.*

That chunk of revenue was also one of the most volatile. Though individuals have to pay some taxes regardless of their income, companies only have to pay taxes when their revenue outweighs their costs. A person who spends all the money she earns still owes the government a check on April 15. A company that does the same thing, breaking even, pays no taxes. Moreover, a company that loses money can use the loss to lower its tax bills in the future and, by a marvel of time-travel made possible only by accounting, in the past. A couple

---

* This figure does not include the payroll tax collections intended for Social Security and Medicare.

of lousy years for corporate America could take a big, sudden bite out of the Treasury's coffers: even though profits fell by just 9 percent, the government's estimate of how much tax companies owed fell by 20 percent.

Already, as Floridians finished counting their hanging and dimpled chads, it seemed like the anticipated surpluses were beginning to disappear. And the news got worse. During the first several months of 2001, the world's financial giants—from Switzerland's UBS to San Francisco's Bank of America—lowered their forecasts for economic growth in that year and in 2002. The Congressional Budget Office did not follow suit, but it agreed that lower corporate profits would result in smaller tax collections.

Long before these ill omens, the Bush team had seemed anxious to believe that the economic situation was worsening. In September 2000, George W. Bush had accused the Clinton administration of leading the nation into an "education recession"—a gap in schooling that would allow the rest of the world to take jobs from young Americans and imperil their future prosperity. In the same breath, he asserted that the big tax cut he had proposed would offer "an insurance policy against an economic slowdown or a recession." The funny thing was, few analysts of the economy then believed that the nation was heading into a recession.

By December 2000, however, the Bush team's rhetoric had solidified. On December 3, about a week before Al Gore conceded defeat in the presidential election, vice presidential nominee Dick Cheney said the economy "may well be on the front edge of recession."* A few days later, after some initial backpedaling, George W. Bush echoed his running mate's comments.

At the time, some experts warned that Messrs Bush and Cheney were actually driving the nation towards recession by making dire predictions. "When national figures keep highlighting problems with the economy, it tends to become a self-fulfilling prophecy," said Edward F. McKelvey, a senior economist at Goldman Sachs, the Wall Street heavyweight.

In the end, the comments from the Bush camp were a little premature—the National Bureau of Economic Research dated the recession's onset to March 2001—but the gist was largely correct.† Whether or not the rhetoric speeded the economy's decline, all those other forces took their toll.

This time around, those forces would also cut off some of the economy's usual lifelines. Businesses had overbuilt their capacity to produce goods and services. Many had recently upgraded their entire computer sys-

---

* The vice president was right, but, since his remark, the president has moved back the date of recession. He has spoken repeatedly of inheriting an economy already in recession. See, for example: Dana Milbank, "As 2004 Nears, Bush Pins Slump on Clinton," *The Washington Post*, July 1, 2003.

† The National Bureau of Economic Research is a non-profit, non-partisan research institution. One of its committees is the accepted arbiter of the dates of recessions and booms in the United States. As it happens, Martin S. Feldstein, mentioned later, is the bureau's president and also serves on that committee, which contains economists of several different theoretical and political stripes.

tems to avoid the "Y2K" problem of dealing with dates
in the new century. Manufacturers, retailers and whole-
salers of all sorts had record inventories of unsold products, worth a total of $1.2 trillion, left on their shelves.
Even if demand returned with a vengeance after a short
lull, there would be little immediate reason for companies to grow.

Making matters still worse, the global economy itself
would provide less of a cushion for a recession in the
United States than it had in the past. Households' and
businesses' appetite for imports had almost tripled in the
past four decades. Money spent on imports, as a percentage of all spending by those two groups, rose from 5
percent in 1960 to 15 percent in 2000. In other words,
back in 1960, a government using a tax cut to stimulate
the economy could reasonably expect that 95 cents of
every dollar given back to consumers or companies
would end up back in the American economy. By 2000,
that figure had shrunk to 85 cents out of every dollar.

The exchange rate would also offer less help to the
economy than it had in challenging times past. Usually,
when the prospects for the American economy dim, and
stay dim for a while, the expected returns on American
stocks and bonds fall. With lower returns to offer, these
securities become less attractive to foreign investors. The
investors use more of their money to buy stocks and
bonds in other markets around the world. Since they
only need dollars if they want to buy American securities, world demand for dollars declines.

There's an international market for dollars just as

there is for dolls or Dalís. So if the demand for other currencies does not fall as fast, the dollar's exchange rate—its price—declines. This chain of events eventually brings good news for the economy's growth. A weaker dollar means foreigners will have an easier time buying things from the United States, and Americans might not buy as much from those same foreign countries.

Yet part of that equation would no longer add up as it had in the past. Some of the nation's biggest trading partners—most notably China and other countries in the Far East—had linked their currencies to the dollar. When the dollar dropped in value, it would affect neither the price of a Chinese toy in the United States nor the price of an American software package in China. Moreover, American companies would gain little advantage when competing with China's industries for the rest of the world's business.

Even though the recession seemed likely to be a shallow one, it was also likely to be part of a prolonged slump. President Bush's advisers would have known this, too. They weren't clueless bumpkins who just happened to have gotten their mitts on the government's economic levers. They were a team of highly skilled economists with their eyes wide open to the vicissitudes of the international system. Yet instead of becoming more cautious in the face of uncertainty, they declared that the shifting circumstances only made their policies more urgently important.

Theirs was a revolutionary mindset. After all, revolutions rarely occur in good economic times. They usually need popular support, and that support tends to be much more forthcoming when people aren't too happy about the situation they're in. But even though bad economic times may be good for political revolutions, they can be the worst times to experiment with economic policy—especially economic policy that's never been tried before. If the policy doesn't work out, the economy can be left struggling for alternatives.

The special thing about the fight for the neoconomy, of course, was that it would not be a case of the people rising up against tyrannical rulers. Instead, the rulers would bring the revolution on the people. They still needed to persuade the public of their ideas, at least to the degree that Congress cared about public opinion. But there was no doubt: good times or not, the revolution was coming.

2

THE NEOCONOMY

If a thousand men were not to pay their tax-bills
this year, that would not be a violent and bloody
measure. . . . This is, in fact, the definition of a
peaceable revolution, if any such is possible.

—HENRY DAVID THOREAU

So what exactly was the neoconomy, and where did it
come from? When George W. Bush took office, the neoconomy was still just a dream held dear by a dedicated
cadre of academic economists. The new president
seemed to set his sights on making that dream a reality
within a decade of his inauguration, or less. But the
development of the very idea of the neoconomy had
taken much longer.

Many of the most powerful ideas in economics—
gains from trade, supply and demand, the invisible hand
of the market, the importance of competition—had
already been conceived before the 20th century began.
Even the ancient Romans were intimately familiar with
the basics of economic policy, whether they were setting
tax rates or interest rates. But it was in the early 20th
century that the injection of academic economics into
government decision-making became truly significant.

John Maynard Keynes set the model. His academic work had suggested that the government could fine-tune some of the economy's fluctuations, rather than being buffeted helplessly by the seemingly endless cycle of booms and busts. In the midst of the Great Depression, he and his theories quickly became influential in the highest echelons of government, both in his native Britain and in the United States. Following Keynes's ideas, Washington's role in the economy grew rapidly in the 1930's. World War II and its aftermath enlarged that role to never-before-seen levels.

Both crises came at a time when economists were just starting to formalize their science mathematically, to codify its theories and test them with copious data. They were eager to flex their muscles.

Following the depression and the subsequent wartime boom, the government's involvement in the economy stayed in roughly the same proportions all the way through the 1960's. Even then, however, the government's choices about spending, taxes and the regulation of industry were still being guided by theories hatched in the 1930's and 1940's, or earlier. It wasn't too surprising, given that those theories were the ones that the most senior economists—those who made it to Washington—had grown up with.

In the late 1950's, many economists began to believe in a negative, more-or-less constant link between inflation—the average rate at which prices rose in the economy—and unemployment. At the most basic level, this relationship was consistent with Keynes's teachings.

More importantly, it seemed like a genuinely useful tool; it offered a formula with which the government could head off joblessness by pumping more money into the economy.

Then came the 1970's. Rocketing oil prices sent inflation and unemployment higher *at the same time,* a turn of events that was inconsistent with the theory. The cost of doing business had risen and, at the same time, consumers had less money to spend after paying for fuel. The traditional theories, grounded in the bedrock of economics for decades, no longer worked for the American economy. They offered little guidance for limiting the damage.

New thinking was already evolving, however. In the 1960's, a group of intensely mathematical economists had begun to develop new models of the economy. These models were just sets of equations that purported to describe how the economy behaved over time. The equations were of the sort that had previously belonged to mathematicians, physicists and engineers; they linked together stocks and flows of labor and capital with functions that could just as easily have described the paths of subatomic particles or the stress levels on an I-beam. Given a starting point, the models could predict how living standards would change as the economy moved, inexorably, to a stable equilibrium.

When the economy reached that equilibrium—perhaps in a few months, perhaps in a decade—it would still be subject to the ups and downs of the economic cycle. But the average rate at which the economy grew, over long periods of time, would stay the same. The models showed how taxes, saving, depreciation and population growth could determine that rate by changing the economy's supplies of labor, capital and technology.

In academia, the focus shifted to the long run. Keynes's short-run management of demand—trying to increase or decrease the amount of goods and services households and businesses wanted to buy in order to smooth out the economy's ups and downs—became a secondary issue. In any case, no one knew exactly how long the short run was. Was it six months, a year, three years, or five? It didn't matter, if you were aiming to increase the economy's potential to produce in the long run.

This philosophy became the basis of true supply-side economics. The new task for government was to procure the best possible long-run equilibrium—the one with the highest living standards—for the economy. So where to begin? In the United States, the size and growth of the population, and therefore the labor force, were generally taken as given. So, at the time, was the rate of technological innovation.

That left capital: all the machines, tools and whatever else workers used to turn raw materials into things people wanted to buy. If the government could encourage businesses to spend more on capital, the economy would start to grow faster. More capital would mean more production, even if everything else stayed the same.

According to the models, the faster growth would not last forever. Eventually the economy would settle

back down to its old rate of expansion. Still, that temporary spurt would make a world of difference. By pushing the economy onto a higher, though parallel, track, it
would raise living standards *permanently*.

What could be done to achieve this leap forward, this
sprint in the middle of a marathon? How could government encourage companies to spend more? One way
was to increase the payback, in other words, the return
to investing. So how could the return to investing be
increased?

To start with, it was worth asking who were the people who received that return. At bottom, they weren't
big banks, giant pension funds or multinational conglomerates—those weren't people, after all. Someone
had to deposit the money in the banks. Someone had to
save up in the pension funds. And someone had to buy
the stocks and bonds of the big conglomerates. By now
you've guessed it: individuals, at home and abroad,
eventually owned all the nation's capital and received
any income it generated. Who else could it have been?
Their pets?*

Clearly, one way to encourage saving by individuals,
which would finance investment by companies, was to
allow the individuals to keep more of the returns to that
saving. Cutting taxes seemed to offer an easy solution.
Taxes affected virtually every type of return from saving:
interest income from bonds and bank accounts, divi-

* Of course not. As Jerry Seinfeld famously pointed out, dogs have
no pockets. No pockets, no money.

dends from stocks and private partnerships, capital gains on everything from trucks to Toulouse-Lautrecs. You paid taxes once when you earned money as income, then, if you saved what was left over, you paid more tax on any more income that resulted. Any dividend you received had already been taxed, as corporate profits, before the company you invested in could write you a check. And if you saved too much—i.e., you didn't die broke—your heirs might have to pay still more tax on your assets.

If you were trying to weigh up your financial options, choosing whether to spend your paycheck today or save it for tomorrow, then all these taxes sat on one end of the see-saw. They reduced the overall return on saving, and could make spending money today relatively more attractive.

Framed in economic terms, these taxes were not only an obstacle to saving but also detractors from happiness. By distorting people's choices about when to spend their money, the taxes made them less well off. Furthermore, one could argue that the government ought to have been in the business of promoting saving, not discouraging it, if only to make sure people had enough wealth to live off in retirement. Weren't there better ways to collect revenue than this mishmash of taxes? This was the question that supply-side theory asked in the later years of the 20th century.

Economists came up with plenty of answers. Most replaced the taxes on saving—the dividend and interest tax, the capital gains tax and sometimes the estate and gift tax—with taxes on spending. Their proposals included a flat tax on wages, a national sales tax and a tax on the value added at each stage of the production process, as raw materials and labor were transformed into saleable goods and services.

Free of taxes on saving, the new breed of models predicted, the economy would flourish. More financing would be available for corporate investment, and fewer profitable opportunities to grow would go unpursued. The economy would expand at a higher rate for a while, on its way to a new equilibrium. Then it would resume its old pace, but from a higher base. Standards of living would permanently improve, and the quantum leap would be complete.

Or so the thinking went until the late 1980's, when another generation of economists added a twist to the models of the previous two decades. Those earlier models had assumed that the rate of technological change was constant or, at least, that it was set by forces that no one could control. This notion did not satisfy the new generation, however. They saw that not all the capital companies bought was used for production. Some went for research and development. Wouldn't it make more sense, they asked, if corporate spending had an effect on the development of new technologies?

They answered their own question by devising yet another set of models in which building up the stock of capital could spur innovation all by itself. These models seemed to fit the data describing the American economy better than their predecessors, at least under the right assumptions. The basic idea, that capital spending could be an engine for innovation, steadily gained adherents in academia throughout the 1990's.

The implication for the neoconomists was massive: the whole saving-and-capital exercise actually affected technology, too! If there was more money available in general, presumably there would also be more money for research. And more research might uncover more of those treasured innovations every year, enough to permanently raise the *rates* at which the economy and living standards grew.

All of a sudden, taking away the taxes on saving offered even more promise. Not only would it give the economy a temporary growth spurt, but it could also continue to push living standards to greater heights for years on end.

Here was how it would work in practice. First, the government would abolish all sorts of taxes on saving—taxes on dividends, interest, capital gains, estates and, indirectly, corporate profits. Next, the nation's saving rate would rise; people would put more of their after-tax income into bank accounts, investment portfolios, retirement accounts, pension funds, businesses, houses and every other kind of asset. This part was an assumption, but it seemed like a logical one. After all, the return on these assets would rise, perhaps even doubling for the highest-earning people with the most money to save.

Then the payoffs would come. First of all, control of a substantial chunk of the nation's income would shift from the government back to households, who could use it more efficiently to improve their own well-being. Second, the economy would get bigger as more and more companies turned households' savings into productive capital. A bigger economy would mean more income to be shared by the nation. And third, more Americans would get back to what President Calvin Coolidge called the chief business of the nation: business.

The first payoff assumed that consumers really could spend money in a way that improved society's well-being as much as the government's spending did. The second payoff assumed that companies wouldn't waste money on perks and poor investments, perhaps as a result of the discipline imposed by a competitive market for financing.

By contrast, the existence of the last payoff rested on a basic tenet of economic theory. It states that lowering tax rates makes people better off not only by leaving more change clinking in their pockets but also by removing distortions in their decisions about how much to work, spend and save. Taxes on wages, for example, drive a wedge between what workers take home and the cost of labor to businesses. In other words, companies trying to hire more workers have to pay more than those workers actually demand in wages, since part of that pay goes directly to Uncle Sam. With lower taxes on wages, employers and employees can split the difference, paying higher wages at less cost to themselves.

The same would go for taxes on saving, which created a disparity between the return investors earned and the amount companies had to pay to borrow. Cutting taxes would mean more transactions between individuals and businesses, more gains from trade and more well-being for all involved.

So there Americans would be, merrily keeping more of their income, merrily saving more, and merrily watching the economy expand more quickly than ever. It was as though the economy would return to a state of nature, before the government imposed all those pesky taxes on dividends, interest and other income from capital. It was a neoconomy: the old made new again.

3

THE NEOCONOMISTS

Every revolution was first a thought in one man's mind, and when the same thought occurs in another man, it is the key to that era.

—RALPH WALDO EMERSON

The idea that cutting taxes would stimulate economic growth was nothing new by the time George W. Bush took office. Several presidents, both Republican and Democrat, used that notion to propel legislation during the 20th century. For example, take these oft-misquoted words:

It is increasingly clear that no matter what party is in power, so long as our national security needs keep rising, an economy hampered by restrictive tax rates will never produce enough jobs or enough profits.

They issued from the mouth of John F. Kennedy in 1962, echoing the idea that in the long run, the economy's supplies of labor and capital would be higher with lower taxes.

In the Reagan administration, however, the supply-side doctrine took a radical turn. An economic adviser named Arthur B. Laffer, along with his fellow gadflies, claimed that cutting tax rates could actually increase tax revenue. In other words, tax rates were so high—so restrictive, to use President Kennedy's term—that slashing them would result in an enormous expansion in the nation's income. Even at the lower rates, the Treasury would collect more money than it ever had before.

What Dr. Laffer proposed was indeed a theoretical possibility. But to President Reagan, it became reality. Weren't tax rates obviously too high, with a 70 percent rate on investment income and a 50 percent rate on wages and salaries in the top bracket? Convinced that they were, he put together a dramatic slate of cuts. And then, in 1983, income tax revenue fell for the first time in 12 years.

All this worried Martin S. Feldstein, the Harvard professor who had become chairman of the president's Council of Economic Advisers in 1982.* A moderate supply-sider named the best young economist in the United States in 1977, Professor Feldstein had wholeheartedly supported the tax cuts. But the changes in the government's cash flow were a source of concern, to him perhaps more than to anyone else.

Just before President Reagan took office, Professor

---

* I was a student of Martin S. Feldstein as an undergraduate and graduate student at Harvard. He was an excellent adviser who taught me many of the skills I'm using to write this book.

Feldstein had, with a colleague, published a stark if not particularly surprising fact about financial markets: people tended to invest most of their savings in their home countries, regardless of the other opportunities available around the world. This meant that if businesses were going to spend more on capital, most of the money would have to come from within the United States rather than from abroad.

The problem was, widening federal deficits could get in the way. American companies raised money for new projects by selling shares or by borrowing. The money they raised came from people who saved. These people bought the shares and made the loans, either through banks or by buying bonds. But when the government needed to borrow, it tapped the same pools of money. So Professor Feldstein wanted to make sure that the federal government stayed away from deep deficits, since financing them would require borrowing money that could otherwise have found a home in the corporate sector.

The budget deficit of 1983 was of a size never seen—more than a third of the government's revenue. Tax revenue wasn't rebounding the way the most ardent supply-siders (like Dr. Laffer) had predicted, and their philosophy was getting a bad name. Professor Feldstein urged Congress and the president to narrow the budget gap, by cutting spending and putting off scheduled tax cuts. He insisted that the deficits projected for the coming years were keeping interest rates high, making borrowing more costly to companies and hurting the nation's prospects for growth. The president would hear none of it, arguing that any extra money received in Washington would simply be spent, wastefully, by Congress. Professor Feldstein was, according to officials quoted anonymously at the time, told to shape up or ship out.

In the summer of 1984, he shipped out.

He kept his message alive, however. Over the next two decades, Professor Feldstein taught literally thousands of students the virtues of tax cuts and saving. Some of those who worked most closely with him, before and after his time in Washington, imbibed the message and refined it.

Two of his best students were R. Glenn Hubbard and Lawrence B. Lindsey. They finished their doctorates at Harvard in 1983 and 1985, respectively, and went on to devote a substantial share of their professional efforts to demonstrating the importance of capital accumulation and how changes in tax systems could encourage it. Like their mentor, they also showed an interest in bringing their ideas to Washington.

Mr. Lindsey had been executive director of Vice President Dan Quayle's Council on Competitiveness, which was notorious for pressuring other government agencies to soften health and safety rules and environmental regulations. After that, Mr. Lindsey was the first President Bush's special assistant for policy development. Professor Hubbard was deputy assistant secretary of the Treasury for tax analysis during the same administration.

In 1991, the president appointed Mr. Lindsey to the

Board of Governors of the Federal Reserve. The year before, he had published a ringing endorsement of the changes wrought during the Reagan administration, called *The Growth Experiment: How the New Tax Policy Is Transforming the U.S. Economy*. As well as asserting the importance of President Reagan's tax cuts, he laid out a program for future growth driven by economic policy:

> The key to economic growth and a rising standard of living is capital investment in new technology, equipment, and processes. But a society cannot invest more than it saves except by borrowing from abroad. America's savings rate is the lowest in the industrialized world and our tax system, though vastly improved since the late 1970's, is still biased against savings. But with only a very modest loss of tax revenue, the tax system can be reformed to substantially encourage the savings we need to sustain our investment in a more productive economy.

A decade later, as George W. Bush was preparing for his inauguration, the American Enterprise Institute published a book called *Transition Costs of Fundamental Tax Reform*, edited by Professor Hubbard and Kevin A. Hassett.* The book contained a collection of rather dry aca-

---

* Mr. Hassett, a resident scholar at the right-leaning institute, had gained notoriety a couple of years earlier by co-writing a book called *Dow 36,000: The New Strategy for Profiting From the Coming Rise in the Stock Market*. In May 2004, the Dow Jones Industrial Average was still struggling to break 11,000.

demic papers all arguing that a major revision of the tax code—especially one that removed taxes on saving—would offer greater benefits and smaller costs than conventional wisdom might suggest. In an excerpt of the introduction circulated by the institute, the editors wrote:

> Many fundamental reform proposals, such as . . . forms of a consumption tax, promise economic benefits by lowering marginal tax rates and by changing the tax base to bypass those areas of the economy that are particularly costly if taxation distorts them. The key sector is capital formation, which has long and widely been acknowledged as especially impaired by taxation.

So what does that mean in plain English? Here's a translation:

> Many ideas for changing the tax system, like a shift to a tax on spending instead of the income tax, promise to make society better off in two ways. The first way is by taxing more people, so that the government can collect enough revenue with lower tax rates. Though some people may end up worse off, society as a whole may still gain if lower tax rates encourage people to work and save more. The second way is by not taxing economic activities easily discouraged by taxation. According to many economists, one of those activities is saving.

The neoconomy had captured the minds and hearts of a tight-knit group of academic economists, among whom Professor Hubbard and Mr. Lindsey stood at the vanguard.* Mr. Lindsey had proposed a dramatic if not complete reform of income taxes. He suggested an expansion of tax-free Individual Retirement Accounts (IRAs). Any investments outside these accounts, he wrote, should be taxed only insofar as their returns exceeded the rate of inflation. Professor Hubbard wanted to go further. In prepared testimony before Congress in 1997, he stated that "both radical income tax reform and radical consumption tax reform are likely to improve the economic well-being of American individuals and families."

The notion, popularized during the 1990's, that taking away taxes on saving could improve the pace of innovation had added another big gun to the arsenal for their long-dreamt-of revolution. But who would provide the troops?

A ready-made revolutionary army came in the form of the Republican Party. For decades, the strongest plank in the Republican platform had been lower taxes—the idea that money was best used when it stayed in the hands of households and businesses, not the government. It wasn't that Republicans spent all their leisure time studying cutting-edge economic theory. It was simply that the neoconomists' utopian predictions gave force to a creed they had long held dear.

The neoconomists didn't have to look far for their

---

* As a recovering economist I can assure you that I have a heart, and I have no reason to believe other economists lack hearts.

Republican allies, since there had been an astounding stability in the group who advised the Republican Party's national campaigners from the 1980's through to the present. At the core of this group was Professor Feldstein. After his stormy tenure in the Reagan administration, he had counseled the campaign of the first President Bush, for whom his close colleague, Michael J. Boskin of Stanford University, served as chairman of the Council of Economic Advisers. Professor Feldstein was also an architect, according to prominent accounts, of Bob Dole's economic plan when the former senator ran against Bill Clinton in 1996. And when George W. Bush took on Al Gore, the professor made his way to Texas to meet with the then-governor.

Since his stint in Washington, Professor Feldstein had remained concerned that Americans saved too little. He worried that without enough saving—both by households and the government—the economy might grow slowly for a decade or more. Frustrated by slow growth, voters might be receptive to hands-on attempts by government to protect, reorganize or control markets— something Professor Feldstein believed would lead to no good.

He summarized his fears in a lecture to the European Economic Association in 1995: "The sharp decline in the net national saving rate . . . may not only create lower real incomes and slower growth but may weaken capitalism itself," he wrote. "The government policies that discourage saving might make the Schumpeterian vision of a shift from private capitalism to a government-dominated economy more likely."*

Professor Feldstein's academic progeny, the neoconomists, adopted and refined this philosophy. What they needed was someone to carry their standard—an avatar, a savior, a leader of the revolution. And they found all of those, and more, in George W. Bush.

He was the perfect match in so many ways. Just as the neoconomists represented the second generation of the supply-side school, so was George W. Bush the second generation of a presidential dynasty. Both hoped to avoid the mistakes of the past. Moreover, President Bush was a former businessman who understood the basic premise of the neoconomy—lower taxes lead to growing businesses—almost instinctively. Consider this repartee from a taping of *60 Minutes II*, the CBS news show, a few days before his electoral victory was confirmed:

Scott Pelley (CBS):
Your running mate, Dick Cheney, said this week that we are on the front edge of a recession. Do you believe that?

---

* Joseph A. Schumpeter, who taught at Harvard after an ill-fated stint as Austria's finance minister between the World Wars, predicted that capitalism would collapse in on itself, eventually giving way to socialism.

George W. Bush:

I believe there are some warning signs that we need to take seriously. And the role of the chief executive of the country, the president, is to anticipate. We need to make sure that the dollar is stable. We need to make sure that we have an energy policy. We need to make sure that there is an incentive for savings. One of the reasons I'm so strong about personal savings accounts and Social Security is help for capital accumulation in the private markets. And we need to make sure people have got some money—some of the surplus back in their pockets.

The future president saw his new job as that of a chief executive officer. To him, running the country was more or less like running a business. And even though he believed that the economy was heading for short-term problems, the main solutions he offered—saving and capital accumulation—were firmly targeted at the long term.* He was a neoconomist in the flesh.

Moreover, once his mind was made up it stayed made up, come hell or high water. He cherished bold-ness. His campaign speeches were rife with confidence and swagger. He cultivated the straight-talking Texan persona, retreating to his ranch to do manly chores like

---

* An energy policy and a stable dollar would do little to fend off or cushion against recession. In fact, the slide in the dollar's value that took place on the Bush administration's watch was probably a better outcome, at least from the economy's point of view.

clearing brush in between electioneering stops. He projected a can-do attitude.

Finally and perhaps most importantly, the new president also needed to prove himself. By his own admission, he had been a lousy student at Yale University and a mediocre businessman. He lost his first election, for Congress in 1978, before finally becoming governor in a state where the governor had little power. His performance there had been middling, from a fiscal standpoint. He enlarged Texas's public debt by more than 20 percent, despite years of budget surpluses, and left the state on the brink of massive budget shortfalls at the time of his election as president.

Some people said his brother, Jeb, had been the family's main hope to take over the White House. Not a few said George W. was somewhat lacking in brains. Yet even when he won his election by only the thinnest of margins, he acted as though he had a truly popular mandate. In short, he had the will to pursue the neoconomy and the die-hard doggedness to haul it into the here and now.

The proof of this particular pudding arrived right after he won the presidency, as he stocked his economic team with a legion of Professor Feldstein's academic protégés. Mr. Lindsey, once his mentor's deputy on the faculty at Harvard, became the top economic adviser in the White House's inner circle. Professor Hubbard, once Professor Feldstein's research assistant, took over his old post: chairman of the Council of Economic Advisers. Among Professor Hubbard's classmates at Professor

Feldstein's lectures had been Richard H. Clarida, who became the assistant secretary of the Treasury for economic policy. Professor Clarida's deputy, Mark J. Warshawsky, was also a Feldstein student.

Professor Hubbard became the hands-on architect of President Bush's economic plan. Mr. Lindsey's job was to explain it to the president, to the president's allies in Congress and occasionally to the nation.

The only big names on the Bush economic team without a direct link to Professor Feldstein were those with non-academic backgrounds—Paul H. O'Neill, the Treasury secretary; Donald L. Evans, the Commerce secretary; and Elaine L. Chao, the Labor secretary. They would play a lesser role in framing the president's economic plan. So would John B. Taylor, the undersecretary of the Treasury for international affairs. Professor Taylor had served on the Council of Economic Advisers alongside Professor Boskin, his former colleague at Stanford University. But he was more of an expert in monetary policy—setting exchange rates, interest rates and the size of the money supply—than in public sector economics.

Yet the rest of the Bush team did have something else in common, something that undoubtedly affected their views on the neoconomy: they were rich.

The people the neoconomists were advising—the ones actually making the decisions—had reason to be especially receptive to the neoconomy. The biggest immediate benefits of eliminating taxes on saving would go to the Americans with the biggest investment portfolios; the more you saved, the more income would suddenly become tax-free. And the administration of George W. Bush was among the wealthiest ever to take over the White House.

Here are some estimates, compiled in 2001 from disclosure forms by the Center for Public Integrity, a not-for-profit watchdog group, of the financial assets he and his colleagues owned:

Person	Post/Department	Low Estimate	High Estimate
George W. Bush	President	$10 million	$27 million
Richard B. Cheney	Vice president	$21 million	$70 million
Donald L. Evans	Commerce secretary	$12 million	$49 million
Paul H. O'Neill	Treasury secretary	$54 million	$111 million
Mitchell E. Daniels	Budget director	$10 million	$46 million

Of course, it's not unusual for politicians and top officials of the federal government to be well-to-do. Robert E. Rubin, who was Treasury secretary in the Clinton administration, had made millions as a co-chairman of Goldman Sachs, the Wall Street financial giant. But the Bush cabinet, in which at least 10 of 14 members were millionaires (according to a summary in *The Washington Post*), was exceptional for the uniformity of their wealth.

The summary of a report by the Center for Public Integrity stated: "Cumulatively, the President, Vice President and cabinet secretaries were worth somewhere between $149 and $434 million. By contrast, the net worth of the same 16 officials from the last year of the Clinton administration was in a range between $14.5 to $45.9 million."

These figures would have differed substantially when Mr. Rubin was Treasury secretary, earlier on in the Clinton years. But even if he had been worth $100 million more than his successor, Lawrence H. Summers, the Clinton team still would have only scraped the bottom of the Bush team's range. Without Mr. Rubin in the mix, the Bush administration was worth somewhere between 3 and 30 times more than the second Clinton administration.

As a result of their holdings, the Bush team probably had a slightly different notion of the value of a dollar than most Americans did. The reason has to do with the added welfare or happiness that a dollar could procure. For a multimillionaire, what does an extra dollar offer? He already has all the money he needs to pay for plenty of houses, cars, entertainment, meals, college educations and more. Even a windfall of $10,000 would not offer a substantial change in his standard of living.

Yet for a family living on the median household income of $42,228 in 2001, the situation would be a striking contrast. An extra $10,000 could make the difference between buying health insurance and risking illness; renting a two-bedroom apartment or cramming into a one-bedroom; buying a used car or struggling with public transportation.

In fact, a person living at the median income, for whom a dip in salary or a lost job could mean disaster, might have a hard time deciding how to steer the economy. She might be paralyzed with the fear that her choices would jeopardize her own livelihood.

The people in charge of the economy in the Bush administration suffered no such handicap. Whether or not their economic plan succeeded, most members of President Bush's team would still be financially secure. True, if the economy dipped into a second recession and the stock market fell deeper, they might lose millions. But they would also have millions left over.*

Several members of the Bush team had made their millions in the top ranks of America's corporations. This fact may have been crucial to the pursuit of the neoconomy, untried and untested as it was. The reason was that the corporate mindset included a special kind of optimism—not unlike Ronald Reagan's misplaced confidence in the power of tax cuts—that could make radical and revolutionary plans especially attractive.

It was called the planning fallacy. Dan Lovallo, a senior lecturer at the Australian Graduate School of Management, and Daniel Kahneman, the Nobel-winning economist and psychologist from Princeton University, defined it this way:

> In its grip, managers make decisions based on delusional optimism rather than on a rational weighting of

* Though not as wealthy as many of the cabinet members, the main neoconomists could probably count on a soft landing. Mr. Lindsey ran a consulting firm in New York that paid him $918,785 in 2000, and was also a resident scholar at the American Enterprise Institute. Professor Hubbard, who disclosed financial assets worth between $2.1 and $7.5 million, was effectively on leave from his endowed chair at Columbia University's Graduate School of Business, where his salary was $301,000.

gains, losses, and probabilities. They overestimate benefits and underestimate costs. They spin scenarios of
success while overlooking the potential for mistakes
and miscalculations. As a result, managers pursue initiatives that are unlikely to come in on budget or on
time—or to ever deliver the expected returns.

The psychology of corporate managers was more ger-
mane to the administration of George W. Bush than to
any other in recent memory. The president himself had
tried his hand at management as chief executive of a small
oil company in the 1980's and a managing general partner
of the Texas Rangers from 1989 to 1994. Richard B.
Cheney, the vice president, was chief executive of Halliburton, an energy and engineering giant, until he
resigned to join Mr. Bush's ticket. Donald L. Evans was
chief executive of another oil company, Tom Brown, until
he became commerce secretary. Mitchell E. Daniels, the
White House's budget director, had been a senior vice
president at Eli Lilly, a top pharmaceutical company. And
before he took over the Treasury, Paul H. O'Neill had been
chairman (until 2000) and chief executive (until 1999) of
Alcoa, one of the world's biggest aluminum suppliers.

These people were used to acting boldly, to leading
by example. Part of the reason wasn't necessarily
overoptimism, however. Studies of the monetary incentives faced by top executives have repeatedly found that
the decisions they make can generate far greater risks
for their companies than for themselves; the structure of
their pay packages, and their labor market, does not

provide the strongest incentives. From their new posts in Washington, these executives stood little chance of losing their livelihoods in pursuit of the neoconomy. For them, it was all upside—the chance to leave a lasting legacy that would, incidentally, help their former and likely future employers. There would be no hesitation; they were ready to take the plunge.

When the entire Bush team finally assembled in Washington—a little late given that the election had only been decided in December—they brought a uniformity of ideology that had not existed there for decades, perhaps since the Ford administration.

Just compare the singular tilt of the Bush brain trust to the Democratic group that preceded them. During President Clinton's eight years in office, he stitched together a crazy quilt of economic thinkers. Some of them were mavericks with high public profiles, like Joseph E. Stiglitz, the feisty Nobel laureate who chaired the Council of Economic Advisers from 1995 to 1997 and became a fiery critic of the International Monetary Fund; Robert B. Reich, the combative labor secretary who helped to found *The American Prospect,* a left-leaning biweekly magazine, and aired his gripes about working in Washington in a memoir called *Locked in the Cabinet* (1997); or Professor Summers, the blunt Treasury secretary who had, as chief economist of the World Bank, controversially suggested that rich countries hire poor countries to do their environmentally dirty work.

Others were academics without much name recognition outside their field, like Janet L. Yellen, chair of the council after Professor Stiglitz. There was Lloyd M. Bentsen, the longtime politician, and Mr. Rubin, the onetime Wall Street whiz kid, both of whom served as Treasury secretary. Meanwhile, some of the biggest left-leaning names in economic policy's academic sphere, like Peter A. Diamond of the Massachusetts Institute of Technology and Alan J. Auerbach of the University of California at Berkeley, stayed outside the government, either by choice or for lack of a way in. Others, like Alan S. Blinder of Princeton University and Lawrence F. Katz of Harvard University, did stints in Washington, but only outside the White House.

These economists had scant links to those who had preceded them in Jimmy Carter's administration. The gap between the Democratic presidencies had just been too long. Furthermore, no single ideology tied the Clinton team together. Most of them had a taste for progressive reforms—ones that might reduce the gap between rich and poor—and disdain for the notion that tax cuts could solve everything. They had a bundle of small ideas, like encouraging poor parents to work by subsidizing their wages and offering tax credits for college saving, but no overarching plan for the economy.

In a way, they didn't need one; in the 1990's, the economy seemed to be doing just fine without a major change of course. All it seemed to need was a little nudge here or there. The Clinton administration had no desire to force the economy to adapt to a sweeping new set of rules.

None of this was true of the neoconomists. They were not content to leave things as they were. They had a clear agenda of sweeping changes to make in the economy. Even though the changes had never been tried, at least in a large economy, they believed that the neoconomy would fulfill all of its promise.

The person for whom pursuing the neoconomy was most essential, however, was President Bush himself. He had witnessed his father's example: appear to do little about a struggling economy, then lose the next election despite sky-high popularity figures early in his term. He could only lose, it seemed, if he did nothing.

4

THE PATHS NOT TAKEN

To wage a revolution, we need competent teachers,
doctors, nurses, electronics experts, chemists, biol-
ogists, physicists, political scientists, and so on and
so forth.

—FRANCES BEALE

The pursuit of the neoconomy was an attempt to kill
three birds with one stone: a short-term stimulus to
smooth out a rough patch in the business cycle, a permanent increase in living standards and a permanent
increase in the *rate* at which living standards rose.

There was a chance that, having aimed at three birds,
the neoconomists would miss all of them. They were so
confident in their plans, however, that they rejected a
bundle of alternative policies, some of which could very
well have made their own initiatives more powerful. To
understand why, it's helpful to consider what those
alternatives were.

Politicians have three options for providing the economy with a short-term spark: an increase in government spending, a temporary but targeted reduction in
taxes and a permanent reduction in taxes. The neocono-

mists chose the last one, a permanent reduction in taxes. In fact, they chose the permanent abolition of several taxes, a critical part of their long-term agenda. But had they truly been focused on helping the economy in the short term, they might have found that spending or targeted tax cuts offered better value for money.

When the government spends more money, rather than just sitting on it, that money does two things. First, it causes goods or services to be produced, which expands the economy. Second, the money goes into people's pockets. It might be the workers and shareholders of a ballistic missile maker, or perhaps the builders of a new community health center. Either way, the people who receive that money are likely to spend some of it, too. And then the recipients of that extra cash will do the same. Pretty soon, if government spends enough, the economy is humming.

Of course, all these people might have spent some of the money themselves if it had been given to them in the form of tax cuts. But that first link in the chain— where the federal government spent *all* the money— would be missing. For that reason, spending can sometimes be more powerful than tax cuts as an economic stimulus: the government can provide raw demand for the things the economy makes.

The government's spending is most valuable, however, when it buys things that citizens need and appreciate. By way of explanation, here are two ways Washington could achieve the same amount of economic stimulus: 1) by spending $10 billion on new interstate highways, or 2) by spending $10 billion on ice cream and then letting it all melt on the White House lawn. To the extent that Americans would use and appreciate the new roads, the latter choice would miss an opportunity to make people better off.

Now, it just so happens that there is a long American tradition of assuming that Congress and the White House are among the most efficient ice cream melters in the solar system. Millions of citizens are sure that they could do a better job of spending money on things that really benefited them, if the Treasury would only return the cash from its hoards in Washington. Yes, these citizens might end up saving some of it, reducing the boost to the economy in the short term. But they have a point—if well-being is what you care about, a smaller stimulus well-spent can be superior to a big one that wastes the economy's resources on things that people don't want or need.

So what's the most effective way to give a tax cut? Because you're aiming for a short-term stimulus, you might guess that cutting income tax rates for a year or two would do the trick. Yet, as the neoconomists would argue, a lot of people might save a big chunk of those temporary tax cuts. Even if the cuts only occurred once, people might want to use them to raise their standards of living for years to come. Would you spend a $100,000 lottery prize as soon as you won it, or try to hold on to some of it for the future?

There is one exception, however. Temporary tax cuts

can be designed to provoke big changes in people's behavior, so that they spend more in the present and less in the future. In New York City, the sales tax is 8.625 percent—among the highest in the nation. Every year, it's traditional for the mayor to declare (with the governor's permission) a week-long sales tax holiday. For a whole week, nobody has to pay sales tax on their purchases. Because 8.625 percent is not exactly chicken feed, the shops tend to fill up. In the following week, however, they might find themselves a little emptier than usual.

These ups and downs aren't necessarily good for business when the economy is ticking along normally, but they can help to smooth out the economic cycle's own booms and busts. Creating a small "up" during a recession, even if it results in a small "down" during a boom, could mean the difference between keeping and losing jobs for hundreds of thousands of people.

Because there's no national sales tax, these targeted tax cuts usually take other forms, like a temporary tax credit for corporate investment. The credit allows companies to deduct profits from their income tax as long as they spend them on new projects, but only for a limited time. The incentive is for them to shift projects planned for the future into the present. The same sort of credit could be given to individuals: allowing people to deduct money spent on major appliances from their income taxes for a year would offer a powerful incentive to buy those big-ticket items. To make it work, however, the government would have to be absolutely committed to taking the tax deductions away after the year had passed.

Targeted tax cuts have the advantage that they do not reward behavior that is not in the economy's short-term interest. If you didn't buy that dishwasher, you wouldn't benefit at all. They also have another advantage: they don't commit the government to a permanent change of policy that might not fit well with the next economic cycle. The downside is that if the targeted cuts work, they will reduce economic activity in the future. But the underlying assumption—easily made in the middle of a slump—is that the economy will be able to afford the dip better then than it can in the present.

None of this mattered in the spring of 2001, however. The neoconomists opted to ignore this last option for short-term stimulus. They tarred targeted tax cuts with the same brush as other temporary tax cuts, which would not necessarily provide similar incentives for businesses or consumers to spend. They insisted that permanent tax cuts were the most effective way to stimulate the economy. Of course, permanent tax cuts also happened to be a prerequisite for the realization of the neoconomy.

The neoconomists also believed that their vision would achieve the two other goals in the long run: a one-time leap to higher living standards, and, quite possibly, a permanent jump in the rate at which living standards rose.

The first of those goals would be achieved by a build-up of the capital stock that would outpace any growth in the population. With more capital to plow into production, the economic pie would be bigger; the United States would generate more income every year. As long as the population didn't grow explosively during the same period, living standards—at least on average—would rise.

But stacking up more capital was not the only way. The economic growth needed to underpin higher standards of living could come from any of the components of the economy: capital, but also labor and the innovations or technology that tie capital and labor together in ever more productive ways. Increase any of the three—labor, capital or technology—and the economic pie will expand. And with all three, an increase can take the form of quantity or quality.

Boosting the quantity of labor is not the easiest thing for government to do. It requires either more workers—from higher birth rates, immigration or participation in the labor force—or more of existing workers' time. The supply-siders of the Reagan era thought that cutting income taxes would lead more Americans to work, or to work longer hours. But the hours worked per week by private-sector employees actually fell, slowly but surely, from 35.4 at the time of Ronald Reagan's inauguration, to 34.3 as Bill Clinton took the reins 12 years later. The rate at which men participated in the labor force fell over the same period, to 75 percent from 77 percent. Women's participation ramped up to 58 percent from 52 percent, but it's likely that social trends played as big a part in this change as tax rates.

Improving the quality of labor tends to be a more attainable goal. In study after study, better education and better training have a fairly reliable result: higher-earning workers. Countless academics have offered suggestions for how the federal government might improve the education of American children through nationwide standards, teacher preparation, reducing student-to-teacher ratios, or improving school environments. But the most important outcome, from an economic perspective, may be how long a kid stays in school.

Academics have devoted thousands, perhaps millions of hours of effort to figuring out how education relates to earning power. The question has received intense attention using the most finely honed statistical methods; researchers have even compared the achievement of twins who went to the same high school, to see whether the time they spent in college affected their later incomes. The answer, on the balance of evidence, has usually been that an extra year in a four-year college can raise wages by 5 to 10 percent.

That increment, though seemingly small, can mean a lot over a worker's lifetime. Take a 21-year-old who leaves college early and takes a job paying $20,000 a year. His wages are likely to grow by about 1 percent a year, on average, after adjusting for inflation. If he had stayed in college for one more year, he might have started with a wage of $21,000. Over his entire career, that 5 percent increase could be worth up to $54,900 to the economy, in today's dollars.

That figure is far higher than the average, all-expenses-paid cost of a year at a private four-year college, which the College Board estimated at $26,000 for the 2001–2 term. The government already picks up some of this tab, both by doling out tax credits for post-high school education and by guaranteeing student loans, which results in below-market interest rates. But there seems to be an economic argument for greater subsidies to higher education; for the student above, the rate of return to staying in school would be well over 100 percent.

Though it may not receive as much attention, there is also room for the government to improve training. Government ought to get involved, from an economic perspective, because the private sector won't necessarily develop workers to their full potential. No company has an incentive to train an employee unless it expects to reap all the resulting profits. There's a good chance, however, that any given employee will switch jobs and companies sometime before retiring. And companies rarely pay previous employers for training costs when they hire away workers.* As a result, companies are likely to under-spend on training, from the standpoint of using the economy's resources efficiently. In theory, the government could help to solve the problem by subsidizing training or by coordinating companies, to make sure they pay each other when they exchange trained workers.

---

* A notable exception occurs in professional soccer, where big teams often support smaller teams' training schools by paying millions to sign their young, promising players.

The federal government has struggled to find a productive role in training the nation's workforce. The Labor Department's Employment and Training Administration, with a budget of about $11 billion, is not necessarily ripe for expansion; academic research has consistently found that on-the-job training is more effective than the publicly administered variety. Separately, the government does indeed encourage on-the-job training by granting subsidies to companies that hire and train people from disadvantaged groups. But the Treasury forgoes less than $1 billion a year for the Welfare-to-Work credit and the Worker Opportunity Tax Credit. And disadvantaged groups are not the only ones where training is probably inefficiently low. For these reasons, a coordinating role might suit the government best.

The returns to education and training take a while to accrue, however. Teaching more science to teenagers, for example, probably wouldn't pay off for at least a decade. Retraining workers for more advanced jobs, then finding productive opportunities for them, can also take time. It takes even longer for the economy to reap the full benefits of their new skills. As a result, focusing on the quality of labor isn't always the most popular choice for politicians, who may anticipate quicker gains from encouraging corporate spending on capital.

Labor and capital do have one thing in common, however. If you add a lot of one without adding any of the other, the returns to the one you added—in the form of production or income—usually fall.

Think of an office worker (labor) using a computer

(capital). Paying the office worker for two hours of overtime (more labor) after an eight-hour day might result in a quarter more memos being typed. Paying for two more hours of overtime (still more labor) probably won't yield the same results—people tend to get tired somewhere in a 12-hour day. Hiring another worker (even more labor!) without buying another computer might help production a little bit, insofar as the second worker can go and get coffee for the first worker, or take over while the first worker visits the restroom. But would hiring a third worker make any difference at all?

The same goes for capital. Buying the latest software packages (more capital) might help the worker to become more productive. A fancy mouse pad (still more capital) might help, too. But giving the office worker a second computer (even more capital!) is unlikely to increase productivity one bit, unless the worker learns to toe-type.

A similar dynamic exists with changes in quality. If you replace the original office worker with someone who has ten years' more experience, the output from that particular position might rise. The same might be true if you replaced that second worker with one who's just as experienced, but has a college degree. But would it make a difference if the worker had a Ph.D. in synthetic organic chemistry? By the same token, you might replace the worker's computer monitor with a top-of-the-line flatscreen model. You might also pop a superfast microchip into that computer. But how much of a difference would this make, if the job was still just word processing?

Changes in quality have the biggest effect when they occur together, for both capital and labor. That microchip would be a whole lot more useful to the synthetic organic chemist, who might be more interested in manipulating three-dimensional molecular models than word processing.

Only improvements in technology would not run into this diminishing returns problem, according to the most widely accepted economic models. The faster the economy spat out new innovations, the faster it would grow. You could never have too many of them. And they could even play off each other, the way capital and labor did, combining to achieve ever-greater improvements in the economy's productive potential.

Gains in innovation would also help to solve two of the economy's biggest challenges at the same time.

The United States was running record-breaking trade deficits at the beginning of 2001, meaning that it was importing many more goods and services than it was exporting. The gap was averaging about $33 billion a month—the equivalent of 100,000 Rolls-Royce sedans, 10 million haute couture dresses, or enough flip-flops for every American to wake up every morning and put on a brand-new pair.* The reason other countries were happy to keep shipping all this stuff to the United States was that they liked what they got in return—dollars for buying American stocks and bonds. The only way to

---

* This assumes a price per pair of just under $4. That's a lot of flip-flops.

make sure the foreigners stayed this happy was to maintain the United States' position as one of the most attractive financial markets in the world. To do that, the nation would have to keep coming up with new ideas for making new products and opening up new markets. Innovation was at the core of this mission.

The second challenge innovation would help with was the outsourcing of jobs to other countries. When workers abroad can genuinely do something cheaper than Americans can, economic theory offers unambiguous guidance: let them. Just as economists favor free trade in goods and services for the benefits it brings both sides, they also tend to favor free trade in labor. But for the United States to exploit this latter trade to its full advantage, the economy had to create new and better jobs for the people whose work had gone overseas. Again, innovation was crucial to answering the question of what those jobs would be.

The neoconomists also asserted that their plans would speed the pace of innovation, perhaps indefinitely. Yet if they truly valued innovation, they were taking a rather uncertain, roundabout approach to it. There are more direct ways of trying to encourage the development of new technologies.

According to economic theory, it's likely that the private market spends too little on research and development. The reason is that the benefits companies reap from R&D are smaller than the benefits to society.

For example, take the invention of the automobile crumple zone, which absorbs the impact from a crash, by Bela Berenyi of Mercedes-Benz in 1959. Mercedes could charge more for cars with crumple zones to the extent that buyers thought they would be better protected in case of an accident. But in a collision, the driver of the *other* vehicle would also benefit from the crumple zone's absorption of the impact. Would Mercedes receive any payment in anticipation of that benefit? No.

After the fact, government might have decided to subsidize the price of Mercedes cars with crumple zones, so that society would realize their full benefits. But Mercedes would not have been able to count on a subsidy when it was setting its R&D budgets in 1959 and before.

Because companies are accountable to their shareholders, they will only shunt money into R&D to the extent that they expect to reap profits as a result. When those profits don't include all the possible gains for society, companies might decide not to develop some truly useful ideas. It doesn't matter how many other people, or companies, might benefit.

This problem is especially common in basic research, exploring the deep questions of physics, chemistry, biology and other major sciences. Unlike in the case of the crumple zone, all the benefits of a new scientific discovery aren't always readily apparent to everyone. Read how one inventor described the initial reaction to his most famous findings:

> The practical value of this innovation was not under-
> stood by many physicists for quite a considerable

period, and the results which I obtained were by many erroneously considered simply due to efficiency in details of construction of the receiver, and to the employment of a large amount of energy.

By the time Guglielmo Marconi delivered those words, as part of a lecture celebrating his Nobel Prize in physics in 1909, the wireless telegraph set had become an important tool for communication in business and the military. More years would pass before radios became commonplace in private homes.

Today, the applications of new scientific knowledge can still be hard to pinpoint. For instance, no one has a ready-made idea for a product using the Higgs boson, a subatomic particle that the world's top physicists have been trying to detect for decades. Yet someday, down the road, someone probably will find a very clever way to use the particle or its properties. No single company is willing to pay for the Higgs boson search today, though, so who can fill the gap? The federal government can, taking the same role as when it pays for the nation's military—something we all might need, but something none of us is willing to finance alone.

Basic research funded with public money has paid enormous dividends in the past several decades. A report by CHI Research, a consulting firm, looked at the volume of scientific studies cited in United States patents granted in 1993 and 1994, on the eve of the high-tech boom. The firm ranked the sources of that research based on how many times their scientists' studies were cited in the patents. For citations in chemistry, six of the top ten sources of research were universities that received much of their funding from the federal government. In physics, five of the top ten were universities and two were government laboratories. In biomedical science, six of the top ten were universities, two were not-for-profit hospitals and two were federal agencies.

No one needs a patent, of course, unless they plan to make money from their invention. Seen from that point of view, the results were even starker. Fully 90 percent of the research cited by companies patenting new drugs or medicines in 1993 and 1994 was publicly funded (about three-fifths of that by the United States). For chemicals, 88 percent of the research was publicly funded (about half domestically); for electronics and communications equipment, it was 76 percent (also about half domestically).

The CHI Research report also found that the number of scientific studies cited in patents was steadily increasing over time. Once businesses marketed those new technologies, all that publicly funded scientific research would contribute directly to economic growth.* But the report did not focus on the question of most interest to economists: for the federal government, does investing in research give more bang-for-the-buck, in terms of improving society's well-being, than any alternatives?

That question has been answered, at least in part, by

---

*In the spirit of full disclosure, let me say that I and both my parents have benefited from federal money while pursuing scientific research.

a multitude of scientific studies (some of them undoubtedly funded with federal money!). The Council of Economic Advisers summarized the results from eight of them in another report, issued in 1995. For a given company, each dollar spent on research and development appeared to yield a return of $1.20 to $1.30 to that same company. But the overall return—to society as a whole—was more like $1.50, because innovations by one company could spawn new products and services in other businesses, too.

Now think for a moment: if you were a chief executive, would you spend more in a specific area if the rate of return were 20 to 30 percent, or if it were 50 percent? Neither one is too shabby, but a higher return usually begets more investment. Since one company's incentive to invest in research and development would depend only on its own profits—not the benefits to anyone else—the conclusion was clear: left on its own, the corporate sector would spend less on R&D than society would choose.

When the corporate sector spends too little, the role for the federal government is equally clear: either subsidize private research, or pay for the extra research itself. The latter choice is particularly important when it comes to things like finding the Higgs boson—a case where a company might not see any return at all in the near future. Indeed, a landmark study by James D. Adams of how scientific knowledge translates into economic growth found that the delay between discovery and payoff could be exceedingly long:

A lag in effect of roughly 20 years is found between the appearance of research in the academic community and its effect on productivity in the form of knowledge absorbed by an industry. Academic technology and academic science filtered through interindustry spillovers exhibit lags of roughly 10 and 30 years each. Thus implied search and gestation times far exceed developmental periods in the studies of R&D.

What Professor Adams was saying, reading between the jargon, was that academic research could take up to three decades to turn into new products. That's longer than most companies are willing to wait. Apart from billionaire philanthropists, only the federal government could fill the gap. But was filling that gap the best use of taxpayers' money?

A study published in 1998 hinted that the social benefits of extra money spent on research might be overstated by as much as half, because a lot of the cash just ended up in scientists' and engineers' pockets. Even with this caveat, however, the likely rate of return to society would still be 25 percent or greater.

The question is whether the federal government can be patient enough to reap the rewards of basic research. Perhaps not wanting to wait decades for an upturn in the rate of economic growth, the neoconomists bypassed a direct pursuit of innovation in favor of the indirect route offered by their tax-cutting plans.

Yet in economics as in many other things, the direct route is usually the best. Robert Barro, a professor of economics at Harvard, has offered one of the best illustrations of this maxim.* Many economists have observed that some companies seemed to pay above-market wages. As an explanation, some experts have theorized that these companies wanted their workers to have plenty of money for nutritious food. Eating well, the theory proposed, would lead to greater productivity in the workplace. But as Professor Barro pointed out, if this was the companies' goal, why didn't they just give their employees free meals?

This type of argument implies that investing in innovation directly, through spending or a targeted subsidy, is likely to achieve better results than hoping for an indirect effect from the encouragement of saving. It's the same logic that explains, for example, why poor people receive some of their welfare benefits in the form of food stamps rather than cash.

The fact that the neoconomists chose to ignore this logic, which they surely knew well, revealed just how confident they were of their plans. They seemed to believe that the federal government could do more to help the economy by forgoing the very last dollar of tax revenue from capital than it would by adding one dollar to the nation's research budget. In terms of a single electoral cycle, they might have been right—innovation did take a long time to pay off. In the long term, however, it was far from clear that tax cuts held the advantage. But the neoconomists had made up their minds; tax cuts, and only tax cuts, would dominate their agenda.

* He offered it in a lecture I attended in the fall of 1996.

PART 2

5

THE REVOLUTION BEGINS

If you want to know the theory and methods of
revolution, you must take part in revolution.

—MAO ZEDONG

In his first year as president, George W. Bush had some
election promises to keep. Fortunately for him, the
biggest of those—his pledge to spend $1.6 trillion of the
coming surpluses on tax cuts—jibed well with the pursuit of the neoconomy. Given that he and his team had
been talking down the economy's fortunes for several
months, beginning with those comments in December
2000 by then-vice-president-elect Cheney, the onus had
fallen on the president to offer some cuts that seemed
like they would give companies and households a short-
term lift.

Yet with no small degree of subtlety, the neoconomists constructed a package that would, in fact, bypass
this short-term goal. Instead they took the first steps
towards the neoconomy. Rather than pushing to enact
short-term measures to deal with short-term problems,

they set out a tax-cutting agenda that would last for a decade and, oh yes, also have some positive side effects for the current malaise. It was like going to the doctor with a headache and ending up with an appendectomy—well, hey, at least you got some painkillers. Soon enough, the pattern would become familiar.

At a first glance, it looked like the government could easily afford a big tax cut in 2001. Forecasters had come to agree that the economy would grow only slowly in the coming year, and the government's own bean counters certainly did not expect recession. Even in August, two months after the tax cuts became law, the Congressional Budget Office released a report stating that "the economy will narrowly avoid recession and recover gradually next year."

But if the first years of George W. Bush's term were an economic horror movie, this would have been the part where the creepy music started to play. It wasn't just that the budget office's forecasts would turn out to be utterly wrong. Some of the tax cuts' massive cost had been hidden in the niceties of finance and the arcane conventions of the budget office's estimates. More importantly, the new law's cost on paper had been lowered by arranging lengthy phase-in periods for several of the big tax cuts, and seemingly far-off expiration dates for all of them.

At this early point in the Bush administration, no one seemed to be on the lookout for subterfuge. The neoconomists hadn't tipped their hand yet, so it was hard to tell what their real plans were. Throughout

2001, the neoconomy was still kept under wraps. The president himself never articulated the neoconomists' vision as a motivation for the tax cuts. In applauding the tax cut's passage by Congress, for example, George W. Bush used a form of the word "save" only once, in a passage about the elimination of the estate tax. Instead, he declared that "immediate tax relief will provide an important boost at an important time for our economy" and that everyone who paid taxes would benefit directly.

This statement left out a lot of people. The number of people filing tax returns in 2001 was about 180 million, counting joint returns twice. Of all returns, a little more than a quarter showed no tax owed. Perhaps half of the population—a group drawn from the young, the poor, the retired, unlucky investors and even working-class parents with big families—could not be called "taxpayers" from the point of view of the income tax. If the economic downturn was hurting them (and was it ever!) any help from the new law would have to come indirectly. They would have to rely on faster economic growth to create more jobs and higher living standards.

Though tax cuts would cost the government money, they did not cost the economy anything. In an era of surpluses, they simply shifted resources out of the Treasury and back into households. So, where was that "important boost at an important time" likely to come from? In the short term, it would have to come from people spending the money that the federal government returned to them, or decided not to collect. A substantial increase in spending was never the neoconomists' goal, however, as a closer look at the new law would make clear.

The Economic Growth and Tax Relief Reconciliation Act, which President Bush signed into law on June 7, 2001, was a huge piece of legislation. It boasted 85 sections, most of which were packed with multiple subsections.

One provision grabbed the headlines, however: personal income tax rates would undergo an almost complete restructuring. A small amount of income—the first $6,000 for individuals and $12,000 for families—would be taxed at a 10 percent rate, rather than 15 percent. In addition, the rates for additional chunks of income would all fall during the next five years, as follows:*

Income range		Rates for Added Income	
Individuals	*Married Couples*	*Old*	*New*
$0–6,000	$0–12,000	15	10
$6,000–27,050	$12,000–45,200	15	15
$27,050–65,550	$45,200–109,250	28	25
$65,550–136,750	$109,250–166,500	31	28
$136,750–297,350	$166,500–297,350	36	33
$297,350+	$297,350+	39.6	35

* I have left the brackets for income levels unchanged, even though the tax rate reductions were intended to be phased in over several years (in the end, as I will later relate, they were adjusted more quickly). The brackets essentially increase with inflation, so leaving them at their 2001 levels is similar to putting all the figures in constant 2001 dollars.

It certainly appears that the poorest people are getting the biggest break in proportional terms. Not so. These tax cuts were a bit like the hall of mirrors in a fun house—nothing was quite as it seemed.

So, how much would these changes, once fully implemented, actually affect the tax burdens for individuals or families? A little arithmetic would reveal the answer in rough terms. Compare the tax owed by people at different income levels, without exemptions and deductions, before and after the change:

Income	Drop in Tax Owed (%)	
Level	Individuals	Married Couples
$10,000	20	33
$20,000	10	20
$50,000	9	9
$100,000	10	10
$200,000	9	10
$500,000	10	10

Looked at in percentage terms, the lowest earners still seem to be making the biggest gains. In absolute terms, the opposite was true. Consider the dollar amounts implied by the tax reductions in the table just above:

Income	Change in Tax Owed ($)	
Level	Individuals	Married Couples
$10,000	−300	−500
$20,000	−300	−600
$50,000	−989	−744
$100,000	−2,489	−2,244
$200,000	−5,489	−5,244
$500,000	−17,731	−17,486

A person making $500,000 got a tax cut that was 59 times the size of the one for the person making $20,000. But economists don't care so much about dollar figures; they want to know about changes in well-being. So, was every dollar really worth 59 times as much to the low earner as it was to the high earner?

It's true that a stray greenback can mean different things to different people. To a low earner, it might be half of lunch. To a high earner, it might be half of the tip for valet parking. The person making $20,000 would probably grab it off the sidewalk; the person on $500,000 might not want to risk getting her fur coat dirty. But if she saw a twenty-dollar bill on the ground, mightn't she pick it up? Or would it have to be a fifty-nine-dollar bill?

You can ask the same question in many other ways: does the person who earns $500,000 a year need to pay 59 times the rent in order to live in a place that makes her just as happy? Or eat food that costs 59 times as much? Maybe the low earner eats a bowl of cereal and milk that costs about 50 cents every morning. To get the same satisfaction, does the high earner have to eat an enormous breakfast that costs $29.50?

It doesn't seem too likely. In terms of tangible benefits, this restructuring of the income tax rates probably offered the most to the people with the highest incomes. The same was true for most of the other substantial provisions of the new law.

For example, the limits on itemized deductions, which allowed people to subtract money spent on business expenses, charitable donations, mortgage interest payments and many other things from their income subject to taxation, would be gradually reduced to zero between 2006 and 2010. In 2001, the limits only applied to taxpayers who earned more than $132,950— roughly the top 7 percent of taxpayers.

Even among those high earners, only the wealthiest would receive the biggest benefits from the change. For one thing, under the old rules, a taxpayer would lose more of his deductions—his ways of reducing the tax he owed, such as giving a share of his income to charity— the higher his income was. But perhaps more importantly, the biggest personal deduction of them all, the one for mortgage interest, was of most use to the people with the biggest houses.*

The new law also raised the limits on contributions to tax-free saving accounts like Individual Retirement Accounts (to $5,000, adjusted up more for inflation, by 2008 from $2,000), 401(k) retirement plans (to $15,000 in 2006 from $7,500) and college education saving accounts (to $2,000 immediately from $500). Since high earners accounted for most of the nation's saving, they would reap the biggest benefits from these changes. The amount of saving and investments that a married couple could render tax-free using these devices would rise

---

* The Joint Committee on Taxation estimated that the 32.1 million people who took advantage of that deduction, by counting the interest they paid on home loans against their taxable income, saved a total of $64.5 billion in taxes in 2001.

from $20,000 a year to $48,000 a year—if, that is, you had the income to save in the first place.

What would happen to all the tax money the government had suddenly put back into these high earners' pockets? Unfortunately for an economy already mired in recession (despite the Congressional Budget Office's belief to the contrary), a relatively small amount seemed likely to turn into new spending—as the chief neoconomists ought to have known.

Less than a year earlier, three economists had released an exhaustive study of saving rates at different levels of income. Karen E. Dynan of the Federal Reserve, Jonathan Skinner of Dartmouth College and Stephen P. Zeldes of Columbia University reported that data from three regular, government-sponsored surveys "indicate that the saving rate rises by between 2 and 3 percentage points for each $10,000 increase in income."* In one survey, saving rates averaged as high as 49 percent among individuals at the very top of the income scale. The implication for tax policy was clear: if the federal government wanted to spark a certain amount of new spending in the economy, aiming tax cuts at the rich would be only half as effective as aiming them at people who barely saved at all, like the working poor.

The three researchers reported this result in September 2000, in a working paper published by the National Bureau of Economic Research, where Professors Hubbard and Clarida were research associates. Each of them almost certainly received a copy.

* The income in question here is a sort of lifetime average.

The neoconomists might have argued that saving would lead to economic growth, too, since it made more money available to businesses for buying capital. They were right, in the sense that saving would turn into corporate investment sooner or later. But in 2001, it looked like the wait would be a long one. Companies were using only about three-quarters of their capacity to produce goods and services; even if they borrowed money or sold shares and received some of the money wealthy taxpayers saved, it was doubtful that they would plow it into new projects right away. Instead of investing in new capital, they might sit on it until the economy's prospects brightened.

That is, except for some multinational companies. For huge firms that owned or were setting up businesses abroad, the tax breaks—and the low interest rates provided by the Federal Reserve, the nation's central bank—would offer plenty of money for overseas investments. These big companies could funnel the money they saved, and the money they could now borrow at rock-bottom rates, into fast-growing economies like China and India. The opening up of the global economy would mean that the benefits of tax breaks and low interest rates would not arrive in the United States until after those multinational companies took their profits home. For various reasons, many of them to do with taxes, the process of repatriating those profits could take years.

Another provision of the Economic Growth and Tax Relief Reconciliation Act was the elimination, by 2010, of the estate tax—a long-cherished ambition of the neoconomists. But it had an effect opposite to what the recession called for. It provided a big incentive for the wealthiest Americans to save more, much more than to spend more. This tax—the tax on whatever bequest someone left when they died—only applied to a few thousand people a year, because all but the biggest estates were exempt. In 2001, an estate had to be worth more than $675,000 to be taxed. The exemption would rise to $3.5 million and then disappear in 2010. At the same time, the tax rate for estates would fall to 45 from 55 percent before being rendered irrelevant by the limitless exemption.

For wealthy people who cared about their heirs, this change in the tax code presented a vaulable opportunity. Much more of their wealth could be passed on to their loved ones tax-free. For example, take a person with an estate worth $5 million. How much would her heirs receive, under the old and new laws? It would depend on when she died:

Year of Death	Amount of Bequest After Tax	
	Old Rules	New Rules
2002	$2,635,000	$3,000,000
2003	$2,635,000	$3,040,000
2004	$2,717,500	$3,320,000
2005	$2,772,500	$3,355,000
2006	$2,800,000	$3,620,000
2007	$2,800,000	$3,650,000
2008	$2,800,000	$3,650,000
2009	$2,800,000	$4,325,000
2010	$2,800,000	$5,000,000

Even in the first year, the difference was in the hundreds of thousands of dollars. By the time the estate tax was repealed altogether, the difference would be in the millions.

It is well-known, at least within the bounds of current science, that you can't take it with you. Where a tax levied at death might have encouraged someone to spend more of their wealth while they lived, reducing or abolishing that tax could encourage saving, at least for people who wanted to leave bequests.* And the benefits would go straight to some of the wealthiest Americans—the people who were the least likely to turn their boon into new spending. Providing more saving did result, the change would fit well with the neoconomists' plans. But it was hardly a reasonable way to jump-start a sputtering economy.

One more factor would reduce the stimulating effect of the tax cuts on the economy: their potentially temporary status. Another much-touted provision of the new law embodied this problem. About 92 million taxpayers would receive one-time checks of as much as $300 (for individuals) and $600 (for married couples) as the new 10 percent tax bracket took immediate effect.

That money was probably worth the most to low-income people. Indeed, they might have spent all of it to get through a difficult time. Yet economists could have

* More saving was not a sure thing, however, as I will explain in more detail later. For someone who wants to leave a bequest of exactly $10 million, for example, the elimination of the estate tax means *less* saving is necessary.

predicted what eventually happened to most of the money: people saved it.

As the previous chapter explained, economic theory would have predicted that a check for $600 would mostly end up saved, if it arrived only once. The theory was right. A study by Matthew D. Shapiro and Joel Slemrod of the University of Michigan found that about three-quarters of the taxpayers who received the checks planned to either save most of the money or use it to defray debt, but not to spend it. If helping people through a rough patch or stimulating the economy was the goal of the new law, it fell flat here as well.

The rest of the tax changes in the Economic Growth and Tax Relief Reconciliation Act were nominally temporary, too. To reduce the new law's cost to $1.35 trillion, the White House and its allies in Congress added phase-in and phase-out periods, as well as one final provision: that all the tax cuts would disappear in 2011, shifting the system back to its old rules.

Did anyone really expect a huge repeal of the tax cuts in 2011? It was hard to tell. At least from the point of view of the estate tax, the sudden reversion could create strange incentives: having one's wealthy relative die in 2010, and not in 2011, seemed like a fairly lucrative plan for a prospective heir. Would there be a wave of unexplained deaths of wealthy elderly people in December 2010? Congress probably wouldn't want to take the blame if the morgues suddenly started to fill up.

But with the economy's future uncertain and the surpluses disappearing, it was just possible that the federal government would badly need tax revenue in 2011. Congress might be tempted to let the automatic repeal go ahead.

From a political point of view, however, such action would be difficult at best, suicidal at worst. As the nation would soon find out, the reversion clauses were likely to be more temporary than the tax cuts themselves. The Bush administration had constructed a neat political gambit for itself and its successors. They could argue for speeding up the cuts by charging that anyone who disagreed was keeping money from the American taxpayer. And any politician who dared to stand by as the tax cuts expired—just as the new law ordered that they would—could be accused of raising taxes!

The timetable for the disappearance of the tax cuts made it clear that the neoconomy would not be a temporary affair, evaporating along with its legal underpinnings. But even putting aside the fact that the cost of the tax cuts themselves was likely to balloon, the $1.35 million figure severely understated their true cost to the government's coffers.

The tax cuts meant that the government would probably collect less revenue in the future, though officials in the White House insisted —à la Dr. Laffer—that they would recoup some revenue even at lower tax rates. With less revenue to pay for all the things the federal government did, the Treasury would need to borrow more. And borrowing, even with the Federal Reserve keeping interest rates low for the time being, was not free.

The International Monetary Fund estimated that the extra borrowing cost incurred by the new tax cuts—the price of keeping the government's regular operations afloat—would approach $500 billion. The Congressional Budget Office called it $413 billion, but noted that the figure could very easily stretch to more than $500 billion.

To be fair, the contingency fund of $1.4 trillion in the White House's initial proposal had included $420 billion for interest payments over the coming decade. But this expenditure was not in any sense optional, given the tax cuts. In essence, the tax cuts were a third more expensive than publicized. If they were held over past 2010, the costs would continue to mount: about $155 billion in 2011 and more each year after that, according to the Congressional Budget Office, unless the predicted boost to economic growth could be sustained.

The total cost of the tax cuts was poised to slurp up much more of the federal government's extra money than even the $1.6 trillion President Bush had originally proposed. Though the budget office had yet to weigh in on the numbers, it didn't take a doctorate in economics to guess that some of the $5.6 trillion in anticipated surpluses had disappeared during the economy's downturn: a lower-than-expected national income meant lower-than-expected tax collections. But what did it mean—were tax cuts unaffordable, or more important than ever?

Democrats clearly held the former opinion—indeed,

it was one of the only ways they could tar the Bush administration for giving back taxpayers' money. Kent Conrad, the senator from South Dakota who briefly chaired the budget committee in 2001 and 2002, released statements almost weekly warning of a dire fiscal future. For example, on June 27, 2001:

> While the optimists among us can remain hopeful for a continued rosy projected budget surplus, we have an obligation to recognize the realities of our economy's performance and factor that into our budgetary decisions. Let the sluggish performance of our economy during the first half of 2001 serve as a wake-up call to those of us responsible for budget planning. Congress, and particularly members of this committee, have an obligation and responsibility to take uncertainty seriously in our budget planning.

In response, on July 19, 2001, Mr. Lindsey said the White House was following the textbook:

> Back when I took freshman economics, my text, the classic by Paul Samuelson, assured me that we would never make the same mistakes again, that we had learned our lesson. The particular mistake I am referring to is the Revenue Act of 1932. Faced with falling tax revenue from the economic slowdown of 1930 and 1931, President Hoover and a bipartisan majority in Congress focused first and foremost on the fiscal health of the country. As Hoover said in May 1932, 'Nothing

is more necessary at this time than balancing the budget.' Their solution was to raise taxes. The top income tax rate was raised from 24 percent to 63 percent. The result, of course, was economic disaster.

Today, we are experiencing an economic slowdown, but nothing approaching the magnitude of the 1930–31 slowdown. But qualitatively the same prescription holds. Proper macroeconomic management requires that the government 'lean against the wind,' or act as a shock absorber. That is what the recently enacted tax bill does, and it is vitally important that we resist the efforts by those in Congress to change course and raise taxes.

These words were somewhat deceptive, since, as a peremptory examination of the tax cuts made clear, they were hardly designed to be a "shock absorber" for temporary economic weakness. With so much new saving built into them, the tax cuts were as direct a route to economic stimulus as a flight from Chicago to Miami that happened to stop in Moscow. Taking all their provisions together, the total amount of new economic activity they were expected to generate in 2001 was $45 billion or less—not much stimulus for a package that would cost almost $2 trillion, all told.

In fact, the word "stimulus" was not necessarily the best term to describe the boost to the economy. It implied that the extra spending would somehow catalyze the activities of households and businesses, causing them to jump into a new state of affairs where everyone was doing more of everything. According to this point of view, the economy was sort of like a perpetual motion machine—the only trick was starting it rolling. Some people referred to this task as "pump priming."

But another conventional view among economists is that a boost to spending will just make up for a temporary slackening in growth. After all, the economy never stops running; it just takes a breather once in a while. When the government spends money, or gives it back to consumers and businesses to spend, it is just firming up demand for goods and services until the economy begins growing again on its own. A better term than stimulus might therefore be "replacement of demand." But replacement of demand probably wouldn't be necessary two or three years down the road, when the tax cuts would still have plenty of life left in them.*

The tax cuts were a bit of a bait-and-switch: the rhetoric said they would stimulate the economy immediately, but, in reality, they contributed far more to building a neoconomy in the future. If the wealthy salted the benefits of the tax cuts away, it would not help the economy in the short term. In this sense, the new law was something of a missed opportunity. Its timing could hardly have been better for the purposes of

---

* A third, heterodox view of stimulus comes from Louis Uchitelle of *The New York Times*. He argues that the smaller size of the tax cuts in later years may cause the economy to shrink, as "the stimulus aspect of the Bush tax cuts thus shifts into reverse" ("As Stimulus, Tax Cuts May Soon Go Awry," November 30, 2003).

replacing demand, as it fell smack in the middle of a recession that began in March 2001 and ended in November 2001. By August, the Congressional Budget Office had lowered its forecast for economic growth in 2001 to 1.7 percent from 2.4 percent.

Yet it was strange to think of the Bush administration as a bunch of Keynesians, though Mr. Lindsey's justifications sought to put them in that category. Keynes advocated government intervention in the economy to deal with temporary bumps in the road—a view that was not always consistent with the long-term philosophy of the saving-as-panacea school. But there the neoconomists were, arguing that when times got tough, wasn't it a better idea to cut taxes more rather than less?

The argument would have made sense, except that Keynes would probably have suggested temporary, targeted tax cuts to smooth out a temporary slowdown in the economy, rather than tax cuts that would stretch ten years into the future. Economists who had been Keynesians before 2001 suggested these sorts of fixes, but to no avail. The Bush administration had its eye on the neoconomy, and the incoming recession merely provided a good excuse to get down to business.

George W. Bush was correct when he stated that the act he signed into law on June 7, 2001 was the first major reform of the tax system in a generation. In addition to its other provisions, it ended a perverse situation that had bothered economists for years: two-earner couples often faced a higher tax burden when filing together than when filing separately. Following a tradition entrenched during the Clinton administration, the new law also served some purely political goals, for example by expanding credits for adoption of children and exempting restitution paid to victims of the Holocaust from tax.

The law—the first big step towards the neoconomy— was massive and complex. But the vast majority of the revenue the government gave up would go towards the promotion of saving and capital accumulation. There were, of course, other options: the money could have been invested in the other two inputs to economic growth, labor and innovation. Improving the quality of the nation's workforce or quickening the pace of tech- nological change might have increased the economy's potential to grow just as substantially as a deepening of the capital stock.

Trying to raise the quality of labor, in terms of know- how and productive ability, might have offered the best chance for success. And because workers could only gain experience by working, the natural starting place was education.

George W. Bush had promised to be the "education president" during his campaign, and the Senate had offered the president a golden opportunity to star in the role he had set for himself. The upper house's Democra- tic leadership added $294 billion over ten years in new spending on education—enough to raise the depart- ment's budget by about two-thirds—in its version of the law containing the tax cuts. Among other things, the

money was intended to improve the teaching of disadvantaged youths and make college more affordable. But
in the negotiations between the House and Senate on
the final version, that funding disappeared, apparently
without any intervention by the White House. In fact,
the House came back with an education budget that was
smaller even than President Bush had requested.

In addition, the White House had suggested radical
changes to the Head Start program, which helped pre-
school-aged children from disadvantaged backgrounds
to pick up basic academic and social skills. The latest
academic research had shown that Head Start kids were
less likely to be held back in school or end up in special
education programs, compared to other kids with similar backgrounds. The program also offered long-term
benefits like higher graduation rates, less criminal
offending, and better test scores—the sorts of benefits
that would someday lead to a more productive workforce. And the reading component of Head Start didn't
deserve all the credit.

Still, President Bush wanted to refocus the program
strictly on reading and preparation for elementary
school. He planned to strip out the parts of the program
that were targeted at social adjustment, parental
involvement, nutrition and health.* With the budget

---

* The last of these parts was recently found to be pivotal to Head
Start's success. See Janet Currie and Matthew Neidell, "Getting
Inside the 'Black Box' of Head Start Quality: What Matters and What
Doesn't?" *National Bureau of Economic Research Working Paper Series*,
No. 10091 (November 2003).

President Bush suggested, the program's funding per student would actually have fallen—another challenge to its effectiveness.

The "education president" was off to a somewhat questionable start. His later initiatives would be more far-reaching but would focus on testing rather than fundamentally changing the educational system. Doing that would have required much more money to help states adapt to new rules and structures.

If labor was largely ignored in the Bush administration's legislative agenda for 2001, innovation did not fare much better. The White House's initial budget proposal for 2002 contained an increase of just 1.2 percent for the National Science Foundation, the main government agency offering grants for basic research (without direct military applications) in fields like physics, chemistry and, yes, economics. That increase in funding was not enough to keep up with prices, which were predicted to rise by about 2 percent in 2002. Perhaps not coincidentally, the White House did not appoint its chief science adviser, the director of the Office of Science and Technology Policy, until October 2001—several months after the new budget passed.

The tiny increase in the National Science Foundation's budget provoked an outcry from the scientific community. One economic argument for a bigger bet on research came from M. R. C. Greenwood, chancellor of the University of California at Santa Cruz and a past president of the American Association for the Advancement of Science. She asked the following question in an opinion piece published in her university's magazine:

> If we succeed in the national goal to improve elementary and secondary education, particularly in the areas of science and mathematics, will the research and development pipeline of ideas that can be turned into economically viable goods and services be large enough to sustain and build the new, new economy or will our students be looking to other countries to provide their careers?

President Bush had not ignored innovation altogether. He supported making some corporate tax credits for research permanent but watched as Congress rejected them. The credits allowed businesses to reduce the taxes they paid on their profits by 20 percent of certain increases in their research budgets, and they were based on a widely accepted economic rationale.

That rationale begins with the recognition that companies can't always collect all the gains from their inventions. For example, the makers of hybrid auto engines probably haven't received a dime from all the people who can breathe more easily thanks to reduced pollution. Nor are they likely to get a check from the government for lessening the nation's dependence on foreign oil. From an economic perspective, however, they should. Because the benefits to society are greater than the benefits to the inventors, the inventors need an extra incentive—like a government subsidy—to realize all the potential of their ideas.

By cutting the cost of inventing, the tax credits offered a small boost to the incentive. And they had shown themselves, in a government study, to be quite an effective stimulant for research. The credits were already on the books for 2002 and 2003. Making them permanent would have cost about $50 billion from 2004 to 2011, the window for which the government's future surpluses were calculated. Though the amount was a fraction of the cost of the White House's cuts in personal income tax rates, the proposal still fell by the wayside. When Congress stripped it away, the White House did not put up a fight.

The neoconomists were relying, almost entirely, on the theoretical idea that stockpiling capital would somehow lead to innovation, all by itself. To judge by their actions, they believed that the neoconomy would do more for prosperity than a direct investment in research and development could. Though the Congressional Budget Office did not compare the two options explicitly, its August 2001 report on the budget and the economy did offer some glimmers of hope for the neoconomists' strategy:

> Many people believe that tax policy can also affect the economy by changing the environment for entrepreneurship and innovation. Recent studies measuring the willingness of people to leave salaried jobs and start small businesses have found evidence suggesting that lower marginal tax rates significantly encourage entrepreneurship. How that encouragement translates into innovations and productivity improvements remains to be established, although some effect appears likely.

President Bush echoed these thoughts at the signing ceremony for the new tax-cutting law, when he said, "Over the long haul, tax relief will encourage work and innovation." Yet as the budget office suggested, the connection was possible—even probable—but still tenuous.

Promoting innovation was an inexact science, any way you cut it. The president's statement was a little like an ad for cologne: "Over the long haul, wearing cologne will help you to find a girlfriend." The cologne might help, though it would be hard to prove in retrospect. The question was, would it ever really be the deciding factor?

Perhaps not, but the neoconomists' approach was the only one the Bush administration was willing to entertain. There were good reasons for this decision from a political point of view, if not from an economic one.

First of all, where encouraging Americans to save could be accomplished with tax cuts, investing in labor or innovation usually required actual government spending. The effect on the government's budget was the same either way—negative—but raising spending by more than a small fraction ran counter to accepted Republican dogma: bigger spending meant bigger government involvement in the economy, or just bigger government in general—a no-no in any area, except perhaps the military.

In addition, when it came to delivering economic growth, labor and innovation were something of a tortoise to capital's hare. Money invested in either of the former would take a long time to pay off, though they would almost certainly help the economy's long-term potential, the worthy goal of true supply-side economists.

From the standpoint of political pragmatism, the choice not to put more effort into education and early development made sense. The economy might not benefit from better education until a generation of kids graduated from high school or college. Why make an investment that might not pay off for years or even decades, when the only election that matters is in 2004? The same logic applied to bets on innovation.

The only long-term commitment the Bush administration was willing to make, on the nation's behalf, was to the neoconomy. Yet even after signing the biggest tax cut in American history, George W. Bush didn't let on. Even if he had, there was no guaranteeing the results that the neoconomists' models predicted. But revolutionary changes certainly were afoot—all those taxes on saving and wealth had to go. The neoconomists' plan was like a checklist; after just five months of the new president's term, it might have looked like this:

Marked For Abolition

✓ Estate Tax
  Interest Tax
  Dividend Tax
  Capital Gains Tax
  Corporate Income Tax

One down, four to go. . . .

6

THE VISION BLURS

It is easier to run a revolution than a government.

—FERDINAND E. MARCOS

George W. Bush, judged by his short political résumé and his razor-thin margin of victory in the disputed election of 2000, might be the luckiest man ever to become president. From an economic perspective, however, he was the kind of guy who narrowly avoided a black cat by stepping on a mirror while walking under a ladder.

Just two months after his tax cuts became law, the president's strategy for using up all those anticipated surpluses was on a knife-edge. He had $3.4 trillion left in August 2001, according to the Congressional Budget Office's estimates. That figure was just enough to cover his $1.4 trillion contingency fund and to pay off $2 trillion in debt. Any more economic problems, and the plan would fall apart.

In other words, the terrorist attacks of September 11 could not have come at a worse time. There's no good time for disaster and tragedy, but the terrorists hit the economy when it was down. And while the shocked nation picked up the pieces, struggling defiantly to push the economy along in the aftermath of the unspeakable, news of other attacks—attacks on the integrity of business—began to seep out.

The scandals that racked some of America's biggest companies in late 2001 and 2002 accomplished something the terrorists never could have: they made Americans question their entire financial system. At a time when almost a third of the federal government's future surpluses had already been devoted to bringing about the neoconomy, those scandals suddenly put the whole plan in doubt.

The attacks of September 11 affected the economy profoundly in its present and its future. In the present, they took a one-time bite out of spending by households and businesses. For the future, they implied lower economic growth until the threat of terror came under control.

After the hijacked planes crashed, the Federal Reserve—in an exceedingly rare dramatic move—immediately tried to counter the damage by extending credit to financial institutions and then lowering short-term interest rates further. The rates eventually fell by 1.75 percentage points in three months. Though changes in monetary policy usually took even longer to filter through the economy, the Fed accomplished two important objectives right away: it kept the financial markets afloat and showed it was serious about doing the same for the economy.

The stock markets fell by about 12 percent in the first week after they reopened, but the combination of the Fed's cheap credit and a surge of patriotism stopped that drop from dampening consumers' determination. Americans appeared anxious to show their resilience by buying new cars and other big-ticket items. Chevrolet even made "Let's roll," the words of Todd M. Beamer as he apparently joined an attempt to overcome the hijackers of one doomed flight, its new advertising slogan. Though the manufacturing sector was still deep into a slump, consumers' willingness to spend may have averted a complete collapse.

The service sector did not appear to benefit quite as much from any patriotic spending, however. The attacks had created a new sense of vulnerability among people who were used to being referred to as citizens of the world's only superpower. For the first time since the end of the Cold War, Americans believed that they might die by enemy attack on their own soil. Even though the attacks occurred by air, travel of all kinds—even simply leaving home for an evening—became less attractive. Home was a place of comfort and security, whether home meant a state, a town or a house.

Airlines and hotels, but also restaurants and movie theaters, began to suffer. Consultants predicted that airlines would carry 230 million fewer passengers over the next five years. As the bottom dropped out of occupancy rates, lodging companies lost $700 million in the first two weeks after the attacks. For an economy so heavily dependent on the service sector, these blows hit hard. On balance, however, consumers' spending still managed to grow by 6 percent on an annual basis—the most since 1998—in the fall of 2001.

Businesses presented a startling contrast. Where patriotism might have driven consumers to spend, it was unlikely to satisfy shareholders who might wonder why a company was making big investments in new projects during uncertain times. Caution became the byword. Low interest rates were not much use to companies already saddled with more productive capacity than they needed to satisfy demand. As the recession continued in the fall, spending by businesses fell by 17 percent on an annual basis.

Though the immediate shock of the attacks would dissipate eventually, some chilling effects would linger. The threat of terror heightened the cost of doing business, both at home and internationally. Big companies installed new security measures for their buildings and supply chains. Some tried to decentralize their operations by farming out headquarters' functions. A few, initially including some Wall Street firms, moved operations out of big cities and into the suburbs. Others sought to ensure the smooth flow of their daily operations by establishing back-up sites that would stay unused except in emergencies. Insurance companies either raised their premiums for terror coverage or did away with the coverage altogether. Shippers also faced higher premiums and security costs for transit by air and sea.

Though the terrorists never made explicit threats against specific companies, their attacks had the same effect as a gangster demanding protection money from a local bar or dry cleaner. It was as though someone had levied a tax on commerce, except that the proceeds of the tax were evaporating into thin air—not used for any purpose except maintaining the confidence to keep doing business as usual.

By introducing a worst-case scenario that had probably never entered the minds of most Americans, the terrorists had also added a great deal of uncertainty to the economy. Would they strike again? Would they strike in the same way? When, and how frequently? It was impossible to know.

For businesses trying to plan for the future, there was only one way to react to this uncertainty: by postponing decisions until the situation became clearer. This response lessened the chances that the economy would swing strongly out of the recession. In the manufacturing sector at least, the end of a typical recession had been something of a self-fulfilling prophecy. When companies began to sense that better times were near, they ramped up production in order to deal with the rush of pent-up demand that would follow—the slingshot effect. Ramping up production meant buying more supplies and paying more labor, both of which would ensure that the recovery really did arrive.

This time, uncertainty about terrorist attacks restrained companies' willingness to bet on a recovery, and they adopted a wait-and-see stance. Some went ahead with investment projects they had already planned, but many put them off. Few were in a position to hire more workers. The unemployment rate climbed from 4.9 percent in August 2001 to 5.8 percent in December. The number of people with jobs fell by 1,553,000 in 2001, while the nation's population continued to grow by about three million annually. A smaller number of workers was supporting a bigger population, and more people were looking for work.

Whatever had fueled consumers' spending—whether low interest rates, patriotism or something else entirely—they also assumed a seemingly more cautious attitude. They may have just run out of room in their houses and garages; after all, you can only buy so many cars and major appliances. But it was a fact: the people who still had jobs and incomes (and 94 percent of the workforce did) began to save more of their incomes.

The saving rate had been falling fairly steadily since the late 1980's, but three forces—uncertainty about security, uncertainty about the economy, and the tax cuts—were combining to push the rate back up. It had dropped to just 0.6 percent of after-tax income in October 2001, but by January 2002 it had risen to 2.8 percent.

This particular development fit well with the White House's long-term plans. In the short term, however, it meant that the economic slump would continue. With incomes relatively steady, more saving would automatically mean less spending.

The effect of 9/11 on the federal government's finances, in contrast to the effect on the finances of consumers and companies, was eminently predictable. Fewer people employed meant less income and less income tax. Less spending by households meant less profit for business, despite wave after wave of cost-cutting and layoffs. Comparing the period from September 2001 through February 2002 with the period a year earlier, the Treasury's receipts from taxes fell by about 9 percent. In the meantime, the federal government's outlays—including the money needed to fight the incipient war against terror—rose by 5 percent for the same six months. The overall picture changed from a six-month surplus of $90 billion to a six-month deficit of $42 billion. And more problems were already worming their way out of the woodwork.

In October 2001, the world learned that Enron had deceived investors, business partners, accountants and regulators about its financial health. The company had dressed up its earnings with the proceeds of deals that had not yet come to fruition, and there were allegations that its executives used some of the company's money to line their own pockets.

Enron had also concealed billions in debts that would surely have attracted the attention of credit rating agencies and stock analysts. It had disguised an amount roughly equal in value to the gross domestic product of Bolivia. The company was a house of cards—hundreds of cards represented by paper subsidiaries, trusts and partnerships—that finally collapsed, pulling its credulous auditors at Arthur Andersen down as well.

More of the nation's leading corporate names followed within months. WorldCom, the multinational telecommunications giant, imploded after it admitted overstating its cash flow by billions and making secret loans to its chief executive. Bristol-Meyers Squibb, Merck, Halliburton and Qwest also confessed to improper accounting that had created a mirage of strong earnings. Several energy traders, including CMS, Duke and El Paso, said they had engaged in the same sort of shenanigans as Enron in order to give their cash flows an illusory boost. Scrutiny from investors and regulators led to allegations of fraud against top executives at Adelphia Communications and Tyco, the conglomerate that had long been Wall Street's darling.

Like the terrorist attacks, the scandals had immediate and long-lasting effects that would present a challenge to the neoconomists' plans.

The immediate effect was a partial loss of faith in the American corporate system. The legions who had begun investing directly in the stock market during the Internet boom, both because of the seemingly endless gains in stock prices and because of the unprecedented accessibility of trading and information online, had been slapped in the face. The framework of rules and regulations that kept companies in line—the one that meant you could believe what you read in a company's annual report, the one that was supposedly the envy of the

world—had not lived up to its billing. It was bad enough
that investors in so many technology companies had
been overoptimistic about their prospects. Now, it
seemed, you couldn't even trust the companies that had
survived the bubble's bursting.

The stock markets survived Enron's self-destruction
and had battled back from their lows after September
11. They showed they could survive twin shocks, especially with the firm backing of the Federal Reserve. But
the dogged spirit wore off. In the first half of 2002, buffeted almost every week by news of another scandal,
the stock markets were in free fall. Through late July of
that year, the Standard & Poor's 500 index dropped
more, in percentage terms, than it had from the very top
of the Internet boom to the end of 2001. Trillions of dollars in paper profits disappeared. Another bubble—the
bubble of faith in the system—had burst.

The sudden disappearance of wealth from the portfolios of America's investors, who had stuck by the markets through the first bubble's bursting and the terrorist
attacks, extended the nation's economic hardship. Long-
term interest rates were scraping 35-year lows, thanks
in part to more rounds of cuts by the Federal Reserve,
and the money consumers saved by refinancing their
mortgage and other loans did help to support their
spending. But the net effect could have been a wash.

The corporate scandals posed a much greater and
more enduring threat to the nation's prosperity than
any recession could. Never before had so many people
been burned by the deceptions of so many big compa-

nies. The argument that these companies were rare exceptions to the rule—an argument the Bush administration repeated like a mantra after Enron's collapse—was harder to believe with each new, spectacular revelation. Recessions have always disappeared, usually after less than a year, leaving the economy to boom again. But how long would it take to rebuild America's trust in its companies and financial markets?

The question was of pivotal importance to the neoconomy. Even if the White House's vision became a reality, and all income from investments was tax-free, there was no guarantee that people would buy more American stocks and bonds. They might indeed save more, but they would have a range of saving alternatives to choose from. A lack of trust, together with uncertainty about terrorism and the economy, could make investing outside the United States more attractive. Plenty of other countries' businesses would be glad to take dollars in exchange for stocks and bonds. American companies wouldn't be able to accumulate more capital until people trusted them and believed in their prospects enough to hand over the cash.

The huge institutional investors that often moved the market would likely behave in the same way as individuals. If their demand for the stocks and bonds of American companies fell relative to their demand for other financial assets—government bonds or foreign securities, for example—then those American companies would have to pay higher dividends and interest rates in order to attract financing. It would be harder—not easier, as the White House had intended—for companies to find money to spend on new capital. Removing the taxes on saving might still make people better off, by giving them more control of their money, but the neo-conomists' burst of economic growth wouldn't necessarily appear as advertised.

The corporate scandals were adding insult to injury. It was already difficult enough to use spending by businesses as an engine for the economy at a time when they needed only three-quarters of their capacity to produce goods and services to meet the demands of the slumping market. By early 2002, it was plain to see that the neo-conomists would have a hard time achieving ultimate success until America—its government, its businesses or more likely a combination of the two—could reduce the "terror tax" and erase the stain of scandal.

In the meantime, the surpluses that could have financed the nation's transformation into the neoconomy were disappearing, and fast. The economy had pretty clearly suffered a recession, rather than narrowly avoiding it, as the Congressional Budget Office had predicted as late as a week before the terrorist attacks. The "war on terror" that George W. Bush launched in a speech to Congress on September 20, 2001 would require more spending by the federal government on everything from heightened security and military operations to financial guarantees for shaky industries and disaster relief. And politicians and the public were demanding closer oversight of companies by the Securities and Exchange Commission and other bodies. That, too, would cost money.

It was easy to see why the surpluses were disappearing in 2001, and how they probably would in 2002. When the economy takes a hit, revenues are not just lower in the years when growth is slower than expected; they're also lower in the future. The reason? Because of the recession, the economy would resume any expansion from a smaller starting point. Even though the budget office was banking on slightly faster growth for the coming decade than it had in January 2001, the recession meant that the annual surpluses would still shrink.

In January 2002, for the first time in four years, the budget office predicted an imminent deficit for the federal government. Instead of running surpluses for ten years in a row, Washington would slip into the red for 2002 and 2003 before returning to positive figures.

The reversal of fortune had several causes, according to the budget office's report. The economy's problems were foremost; they would subtract almost $1 trillion from the previously estimated surpluses for the years 2002 to 2011. This hit would more than exhaust the $841 billion component of the White House's contingency fund that had been intended as a true rainy day fund, rather than as a kitty for paying interest on the national debt. In fact, between the interest cost of the tax cuts and the economy's problems, all of the Bush administration's supposed wiggle room had disappeared.

At the same time as revenues fell, spending was climbing. The budget office estimated that spending on the military would rise by $301 billion over the decade, accounting for half of the overall increase in the federal government's outlays. Much of that total had been lumped on after September 11. This new spending would offer some stimulus to the economy, but it would not necessarily improve standards of living. The military operations and hardware it paid for would essentially serve to make people feel as safe as they had before September 11, when no one knew what tragedy lay ahead. The same was true for all the spending on security and insurance. Sure, it helped people who worked or invested in those two industries, but it would do nothing for economic growth. It just meant that Americans had less to spend on other things.

Thanks to these factors and some technical changes in the forecasts, the total amount of the surpluses anticipated for 2002 through 2011 plunged from $3.4 trillion, as of the previous August, to $1.6 trillion. In just four months, the United States government had lost $1.8 trillion. The size of the drop in the surpluses eclipsed the size of the 2001 tax cuts. There wasn't enough left to pay down the nation's debts as the president had planned, let alone to tick any more taxes off the neoconomists' checklist. But that would not stop them from trying.

The neoconomists had clearly decided that debt reduction, too, paled in importance relative to their plans for more tax cuts. And this decision took them to one of the biggest forks in the road of economic policy.

There were two ways to react to the adversity facing the economy. One was to reconsider expensive plans for the economy's future and focus on fixing the present. The other was to insist on the future itself as a cure for the present—the idea that giving the nation something good to look forward to would speed along an economic recovery. It was a classic choice between a bird in the hand and two in the bush, or, in this case, two in the Bush administration's plan for the economy.

The White House preferred the latter, taking the risk that the economic languor might continue for a while. An extended period of stagnation would present an undeniable threat to George W. Bush's re-election chances. But for the neoconomists, it would offer something of an opportunity.

In a weak economy, they could keep using the banner of short-term stimulus as an excuse to push through their long-term plans. In fact, as long as they doled out that stimulus only in dribs and drabs, the economy would keep coming back for more. There weren't any alternatives, since nobody else's policies had enough support in Congress to become law.

In the meantime, however, millions of Americans were losing their jobs. Payrolls had shrunk by almost 2 million, just in the seven months between the signing of the tax cuts and the budget office's prediction of deficits. For the jobless, the economy probably felt like a desert, where the neoconomists were handing out water with an eyedropper.

7

FINANCING REVOLUTION

The revolutionary spirit is mighty convenient in
this, that it frees one from all scruples . . .

—JOSEPH CONRAD

Like all revolutions, the one intended to bring about the
neoconomy needed money. Unlike most revolutions,
this one gained much of its financing from millions of
the people on whom the revolution was being imposed.

The core of the revolution, the abolition of taxes,
would cost the federal government money, at least in
the short term. If the government was planning to keep
spending at the same rate—and indeed, Congress
seemed unwilling to restrain itself—then two consequences were inevitable: the expected budget surpluses
would disappear, and the Treasury would need to borrow more.

During his presidential campaign in 2000, George W.
Bush liked to talk about the surpluses as though they
had already been collected, even though they were only
projections for the future. "The surplus is indicative of

the fact that you were overcharged," he said at an appearance at a school in Appleton, Wisconsin a week before the election. At a rally in Chattanooga, Tennessee on the day before the election, he said, "I want to send some of that surplus back to you. But that's no big deal, it's your money to begin with." Yet no one could "send back" surpluses that did not yet exist.

Indeed, none of the $5.6 trillion in surpluses President Bush referred to in his original fiscal plan actually existed at the time of his inauguration. If they really did appear as predicted, the Treasury would not finish collecting them until 2011. No, back in January 2001 the government had only collected surpluses of $431 billion, from the three years that the Clinton administration spent in the black. This was the only "overcharging," if one could call it that, which had occurred.

In fact, American taxpayers had been undercharged, if anything, for all their government's operations since 1969. It was during that period that the nation built up its trillions of dollars in debts. Not until 1998—the first time in three decades—did the federal government finally have money left over at the end of the year.

By the time President Bush took office, the $431 billion in surpluses collected in 1998, 1999 and 2000 were gone; President Clinton had used the money to pay down the federal government's debts. Almost all of the surpluses had come from the Social Security program, which had been collecting extra money through its payroll tax in order to prepare for the baby boomers' retirement. Using the Social Security surpluses to reduce the overall debt probably did help to preserve the program's future. When the program finally started to run its own deficits, a day that the Social Security trustees predicted would come in 2015, the federal government would have to borrow to shore it up. Having fewer other debts to worry about at that point was likely to be a good thing.

In early 2002, the Congressional Budget Office still expected $1.6 trillion in surpluses to crop up in the coming decade. Clearly, that was not enough to allow President Bush to keep his pledge—part of that first fiscal plan—to reduce the nation's debt by $2 trillion. But it was something. Reducing the national debt was not an explicit requirement for the neoconomy, though. So would he bother at all?

Paying down debt certainly sounds like a good idea in general. It's the sort of thing responsible people do. But responsible people usually retire at some point, stop earning a salary and eventually die. For them, there are very good reasons for paying off debts before any of those things happen. The federal government, however, never retires, never stops collecting taxes—its income— and has not shown any signs of dying since the Civil War ended in 1865. So why should it ever reduce its debt, instead of just rolling it over forever?

There's no implicit reason for the government to reduce its debt to zero as long as two things are true: 1) people are willing to lend it money, and 2) spending that money creates otherwise unattainable benefits to the nation that are greater than the costs of paying the interest on the debt. As the existence of loan sharks goes to show—and the world of international finance is filled with them—people are almost always willing to loan out their money as long as the interest rate is high enough. So the more interesting question has to do with point No. 2: when does the burden of the government's debt outweigh its own usefulness?

Countries like Argentina, Mexico and Russia found out the answer in the most extreme fashion when, at various times in the past decade, they were unable to make their interest payments to lenders on time. Their failures to pay led to financial crises and deep economic slumps, as they lost the confidence of foreign investors. To become credit-worthy again, they had to cut government spending and devalue their currencies—actions that damaged living standards in the short term.

The United States was far from slipping into such a nightmarish situation in early 2002. The Treasury's bonds were still regarded by many investors as the safest widely available securities in the world. In fact, one could almost argue that the Treasury provided a service—at little cost to the nation—by circulating its reliable IOUs in an eager marketplace. Foreign governments loved to hold them as proof they could back up their own currencies with reliable assets. Even better, the Treasury's IOUs came in all different flavors, with terms ranging from a month to 30 years. As such, they offered a useful way to balance a portfolio's exposure to risk over time. When, on Halloween Day of 2001, the Treasury announced that it had no plans ever to issue any more 30-year bonds, investors and foreign central banks rushed to buy the ones that were still on the market.

The small deficits projected in January 2002 by the Congressional Budget Office for the next two years would add only a few gallons to the swimming pool of the nation's outstanding debt. The Bush administration could easily make the argument that the deficits were a small price to pay for an economic recovery. But some critics were already warning of disaster.

They took up the same argument that Professor Feldstein had used two decades earlier. Investors in the United States and abroad had a fixed amount of money for buying stocks, bonds and other securities. Every time the Treasury borrowed $1,000 by selling a bond, note or bill, it was $1,000 less that could go towards financing new economic activity in the private sector. Not that the money *would* necessarily have gone to the private sector; it could have gone to a foreign government, or into a cookie jar. But if the Treasury managed to tempt the owner of that $1,000 to trade it for an IOU, then it would certainly not end up in the hands of, say, General Motors.

In loose terms, the Treasury was adding to the overall demand for investors' money when it tried to borrow more. And with investors' money in fixed supply, an increase in demand would raise the price of borrowing: the interest rate.

There's nothing wrong with higher interest rates if you're a wealthy heiress living on investment income without lifting a finger. But if you're a consumer or a company, rising rates can make your plans more costly. A prospective homeowner looking for a 30-year mortgage might be able to borrow $200,000 from a bank at an interest rate of 7 percent. But what if the Treasury suddenly decided to sell $100 billion in new, ten-year notes? It sounds like a completely different market, but there is a relationship. The Treasury's action will probably push up interest rates for corporate and government bonds with terms of around three years. With higher rates available, investors might shift some of the money in their portfolios towards that part of the market, and away from other investments like stocks, precious metals, short-term debt and, yes, even bank accounts and certificates of deposit. If the supply of money to your bank drops as a result of the Treasury's action, and the total amount people want to borrow does not change, then you may find yourself paying a higher interest rate than 7 percent on that mortgage.

This chain of events may sound a bit far-fetched at a time when money moves all over the globe with the tap of a computer key. It might make sense in a closed economy with only a few entities trying to borrow money, but, with so much cash sloshing around the world, how could the federal government's debts be so directly connected to a consumer's bank loan? Indeed, an updated version of Professor Feldstein's earlier research suggested that the homeward bias in people's portfolio choices was beginning to dissipate. Yet it was precisely the interconnectedness of the financial markets that strengthened the premise: a butterfly's wings flapping in the Treasury note market would be felt immediately, if infinitesimally, in every other market in the world.

Back in January 2001, the federal government had owed investors about $3 trillion. The budget office had predicted that so much debt would be paid off by 2011, however, that just $818 billion would remain. But just a year later, the budget office estimated that the amount of debt left unpaid in 2011 would be $1.9 trillion. The rapid disappearance of the surpluses meant that the Treasury would, all other things equal, need to borrow much more in the coming decade than investors might have predicted only a year before. If the Treasury was borrowing, there was no way it could pay off debt. But would the extra borrowing put enough pressure on the market to push up interest rates?

Democrats in Congress and several economists on Wall Street said it would, and they had some circumstantial evidence to make their case. During that same January-to-January period, the Federal Reserve had lowered short-term interest rates by 4.75 percentage points, a huge change. Yet long-term rates—the kind you pay on mortgages, tuition loans and car loans or receive on government and corporate bonds—had only slipped by about 1.2 percentage points. In real terms, the discrepancy between short and long rates stayed wider for longer than it had in the 1990's, when the Fed cut short-term rates while the budgetary situation was stable and improving.

Economists from academia and Wall Street debated the point back and forth, marshalling evidence from past studies, none of which was entirely conclusive. Most of the studies agreed that expectations for the future state of the government's books mattered more than the present year's surplus or deficit. But their estimates of the effect of those expectations on current long-term interest rates ranged from minuscule to immense. Some economists said the expected deficits weren't big enough to make a difference. A few protested that there simply was no reliable link, studies or no studies.

Part of the explanation for the disjoint between past studies and what present economists were saying might have been due to that same interconnectedness of the world's financial markets. The more woven together the markets were, the more the effects of a bigger federal debt would be diffused around the globe rather than showing up solely at home. So perhaps mortgage rates wouldn't be quite so high in the United States; instead, they'd just be a little bit higher in the United States, Germany, France and a slew of other countries.

Another possible reason why long-term rates hadn't dropped had to do with expectations for the economy itself. If the economy recovered fairly soon, companies would again be eager to spend money on new projects. To finance those projects, they would have to borrow money for long periods—that is, periods long enough so that repayment could wait until the projects earned profits. Investors, therefore, could expect strong demand for their money in the near future, and reasonably high long-term interest rates as a result.

Given this expectation, why would any investor lend out his money for a long period at a low interest rate? Perhaps he'd do it for a short period, just to hedge his bets. But locking in a low interest rate for a long time just wouldn't make sense if higher rates were on the way. Higher long-term rates expected in the future would mean higher long-term rates in the present, too.

Clearly, the squeeze on the government's wallet was not the only explanation for the lack of movement in long-term interest rates. Alan Greenspan, the chairman of the Federal Reserve, acknowledged the importance of both factors in a speech he gave in San Francisco on January 11, 2002. He pointed out that a climb in long-term rates had dulled the stimulating effect on the economy of the Fed's string of interest-rate cuts. "The recent rise in these rates largely reflects the perception of improved prospects for the U.S. economy," he said. "But over the past year, some of the firmness of long-term interest rates probably is the consequence of the fall of projected budget surpluses and the implied less-rapid paydowns of Treasury debt."

What did this mean for the neoconomy? If higher long-term interest rates were *not* a result of expectations for a quick recovery, then the news was not good: the government's budget deficits were keeping the economy on the ropes. But if higher long-term rates did signal "improved prospects," then tax revenues would soon be rising, buoying those budget surpluses and helping to fund the neoconomists' plans.

Meanwhile, Kent Conrad, the chairman of the Senate Budget Committee, seized on Mr. Greenspan's remarks in hearings held in Washington a couple of weeks later. A few other Democrats even suggested repealing some of the previous year's tax cuts. The Bush administration, however, was unapologetic. Paul H. O'Neill, the Treasury secretary, asserted that the recovery was on the way—proof that the Keynesian recipe for smoothing out the economy's bumps worked. "Some would suggest that we need surpluses to improve our economy," he said in testimony before the budget committee in February. "They have the logic backwards. Growth creates surpluses, not the other way around."

These remarks were a strong hint that the Bush administration was ready to take the next steps towards the neoconomy, and, in parallel, the next steps into debt. Perhaps the critics would be proven wrong, and the deficits would not lead to higher interest rates. Still, someone would have to take care of the government's existing debts, which would not be paid off as George W. Bush had originally planned, and also the new debts that more tax cuts would create. Who would pay for them?

Future generations would pay. Current taxpayers would have to pay interest on the debts, of course, but there was no chance of paying off the principal until the government began running surpluses again. Even then, the bulk of the debt was likely to be rolled over for many more years. The taxpayers who eventually ended up holding the hot potato of unpaid debt, when all those creditors finally came calling, would not be the only ones to suffer. To the extent that the government's demand for cash weighed on the private sector, borrowing would remain more difficult for businesses around the world.

For politicians focused on two-, four- or six-year electoral cycles, it's an easy call to shift the burden of debt onto hundreds of millions of unborn American citizens and, to a lesser extent, foreigners. In 2002, Congress and the White House were just heeding the dictates of that great economist, Adam Smith, by following their self-interest. None of those unborn taxpayers would be voting in the next election. And no politician seemed to care about their welfare anywhere near as much as he cared about his own.

8

THE NEOCONOMISTS IN RETREAT

When one makes a revolution, one cannot mark
time; one must always go forward—or go back.

—VLADIMIR ILYICH LENIN

The neoconomists had justified the 2001 tax cut with
two rationales: 1) that the nation could afford a big tax
cut and 2) that the nation needed the tax cut to smooth
the way out of its economic slump. In the background,
of course, was a third rationale: that the tax cuts were
the best way to help the economy use its resources efficiently. But when it came time for President Bush to
present his second budget, in February 2002, the first
two arguments had become somewhat dated, and the
third was still receiving little emphasis. He and the neoconomists had, for a little while at least, painted themselves into a corner.

The idea that the nation could afford an across-the-
board cut in income tax rates had been relatively
uncontroversial when George W. Bush took office in
January 2001. By the time the tax cuts actually made it

to the president's desk, in June, some budget hawks in Washington had begun to worry about the effect of the stock markets' decline on the economy. With lower corporate profits, tax receipts would fall short of the rosy estimates made at the beginning of the year. But talk of shrinking surpluses was not enough to slow the cuts' momentum—at least, not then.

By January 2002, the situation had changed dramatically. Fully $4 trillion of the $5.6 trillion in surpluses predicted a year earlier had disappeared, according to the Congressional Budget Office's estimates. The budget office chalked up just under a quarter of this change to purely economic factors—the effects of the terrorist attacks and the deflating of the bubble in the financial markets. Slightly more than a quarter corresponded to unexpected increases in spending and technical changes in the forecasts. The rest of the blame went to the tax cuts and the related costs of deepening the government's debts.

One year into the Bush administration, it would have been a stretch to claim, unequivocally, that the federal government could afford another tax cut of the same size as the one passed in 2001. Only a few months after the terrorist attacks, no one knew whether more trouble was on the way. Further attacks would undoubtedly lead to more spending for security and disaster relief. They would also weaken the government's borrowing position; both the danger of future red ink and, perhaps, the direct threat to the rule of law would make investors leery of Treasury bonds. Foreign central banks looking for a safe way to hold their reserves might look elsewhere, too. Bonds denominated in euros and backed by the European Central Bank would become relatively more attractive, for instance.

A parallel scenario would unfold in the American financial markets in the event of another wave of attacks. Investors looking for a profitable return would have to think twice. After all, would you put money into a company whose headquarters might be reduced to rubble tomorrow, or whose supply chain might become tangled in a flock of grounded airplanes? The uncertainty implied by terror would push stock prices down and interest rates up. Higher financing costs for companies looking to invest in new projects would lead to lower profits, and less revenue for the federal government.

Such were the uncertainties plaguing the nation in early 2002. President Bush was certainly aware of them. He conflated the plight of the economy and the fight against terror in a series of appearances across the nation—but he wasn't just talking about uncertainty. He insisted that Congress respond to his tax-cutting proposals with the same unanimity it showed in backing the war on terror. "We ought to come together," he said after returning from a swing through California and Oregon. "We ought to unify around some sensible policy, and not try to play politics with tax relief."

But against the backdrop of uncertainty, could the nation afford another blockbuster tax cut? The words of Alan Greenspan, the chairman of the Federal Reserve,

offered a barometer for the mood of the financial establishment.* Back in January 2001, he had implicitly
given his blessing to the first wave of tax cuts a few days
after President Bush's inauguration, in testimony before
the Senate Budget Committee:

> In general, as I have testified previously, if long-term
> fiscal stability is the criterion, it is far better, in my
> judgment, that the surpluses be lowered by tax reduc-
> tions than by spending increases. . . . Starting that
> process sooner rather than later likely would help
> smooth the transition to longer-term fiscal balance.
> And should current economic weakness spread beyond
> what now appears likely, having a tax cut in place may,
> in fact, do noticeable good.

But when he addressed the same committee exactly
one year later, he sounded cautious, noting the reversal
of the "fiscal bonanza":

> The fiscal pressures that will almost surely arise after
> 2010 will be formidable. Achieving a satisfactory
> budget posture will depend on ensuring that new ini-
> tiatives are consistent with our longer-run budgetary
> objectives. Indeed, as you craft a budget strategy for
> coming years, you might again want to consider provi-
> sions that, in some way, would limit tax and spending

* In fact, he often set the mood of the financial establishment with
his words.

initiatives if specified targets for the budget surplus and federal debt were not satisfied.

To President Bush, however, the issue of affordability—whether those "longer-run budgetary objectives" were compatible with more tax cuts—didn't really exist. He declared, after a meeting with Mr. Greenspan, that the nation was mired in such a crisis that the government could ignore its balance sheet, at least for a while: "I said to the American people that this nation might have to run deficits in time of war, in times of national emergency, or in times of a recession. And we're still in all three." He called it the "trifecta" more than a dozen times as he spent weeks campaigning for Republican candidates around the country in the first half of 2002. The line never failed to get a laugh.

With affordability moot, the logical next question was whether the economy actually needed more tax cuts. As far as dealing with a relatively mild recession was concerned, Congress and the Federal Reserve had already added plenty of fuel to the economy's fire.

The first tax cuts had arrived fortuitously, just a few months after the recession began, pumping $45 billion into the economy in 2001 in addition to their longer-term effects. The stimulus was small relative to the total package, but it was there.

The Fed's yearlong spate of rate cuts had lasted through December 2001, and economists expected their helpful effects to continue percolating through the economy until at least the summer of 2002. Mortgage rates were at their lowest levels in more than three decades, and it seemed like even an orangutan in diapers could buy a car with zero-percent financing. Refinancing of mortgages—whereby homeowners lowered their monthly payments by locking in lower interest rates—had funneled about $100 billion into the economy in 2001 and was expected to add $50 billion more in 2002. There would be more zero-percent financing deals on cars and trucks, more refinancing of home mortgages and more spending on credit for months to come.

For these reasons, in large part, prognosticators on Wall Street and in Washington expected the economy to grow solidly, if not rapidly, in 2002. To anyone who was even a little bit forward-looking, economic weakness could no longer offer much justification for more tax cuts. The economy still faced uncertainty related to terrorism, to be sure, but dealing with that problem was the job of the military and the soon-to-be-created Department of Homeland Security. The neoconomists were in for a tough slog.

That didn't mean they wouldn't try. On October 11, 2001, Bill Thomas, the chairman of the Ways and Means Committee, had introduced the Economic Security and Recovery Act to the Republican-controlled House. The symbolism of taking action a month to the day after the terrorist attacks was deliberate, though it was somewhat misplaced. To be sure, the bill did include some economic aid for New York City and other people and places affected by the attacks. But the rest of the bill, whose principles President Bush had endorsed a week earlier, provided only indirect ways to counter any economic damage the hijackings caused.

First of all, rather than immediately trying to replace the bite the terrorists had taken out of the economy, the Economic Recovery and Security Act's provisions were to be phased in during the coming four years. The Congressional Budget Office and the Joint Committee on Taxation estimated that the bill's provisions would cost $216 billion in the coming three years; after that, the economic growth the bill might generate would reduce the cost to a still-substantial $162 billion between 2002 and 2011.

The guts of the bill had the neoconomists' fingerprints all over them. The bill contained a raft of provisions all designed to bolster corporate profits and cut the cost of capital. Businesses would be able to deduct the value of aging hardware from their tax burdens more quickly than before. The alternative minimum tax on corporate profits, which ensured that companies could not dodge their entire tax obligation through deductions and loopholes, would be repealed completely.

By reducing the tax companies would pay on their profits, these two changes would take small steps towards the neoconomists' goals. Money not taken away from businesses as taxes would become available to finance new investment. In addition, companies would be able to pay slightly higher returns to their investors. But companies could also retain the untaxed profits, saving them for a day when better opportunities to invest were available.* If their employees had enough bargaining power—as the United Auto Workers union might with Ford Motor Company, for example—a company might have to pay out the extra profits as wages. If the bargaining power lay with the company's customers, as it might in the case of Raytheon, the big military contractor, and the federal government, then the extra profits might be siphoned off in the form of lower prices.

No one has ever completely understood the effects of the tax on corporate profits. But you could predict, with a reasonable degree of certainty, that cutting the tax this way was unlikely to lead to more hiring by companies in the very short term. Since the tax only applied to profits—the amount left over after the company had already done its best to earn as much as it could—there was no reason for the company to expand its payrolls immediately after a tax cut. There would not be any more jobs until the beneficiaries of the tax cut, whose identities were difficult to predict, turned their gains into new spending.

The bill also sought to lower the tax rates on long-term capital gains by individuals, from 10 and 20 percent, depending on one's regular income tax bracket, to 8 and 18 percent—yet another step towards eliminating all taxes on saving and capital accumulation. It was a

---

* Or, according to some theories of the corporation, the money could be wasted on perks for executives.

symbolic step, too; the rates on capital gains hadn't been so low since the Great Depression.

While the government would be grabbing less of taxpayers' gains, it would be soaking up a larger share of their losses. For years, the rules had allowed taxpayers to make their incomes look smaller by subtracting a certain amount of their capital losses. That amount would rise, providing a bigger subsidy to investors than it ever had before. As a form of insurance for saving, it could also have encouraged Americans to make unduly risky investments.

The neoconomists were pursuing the neoconomy from all directions. But, crucially, virtually all of the policies bundled together in the bill were designed for a long-term payoff: the extra economic growth, and therefore income, that would be generated by cheaper financing and a bigger stock of capital. In trying to convince politicians and the public to go along, however, the neoconomists and their cohorts once again emphasized a perceived need for short-term stimulus. As Chairman Thomas said on October 12, 2001, "The Economic Security and Recovery Act of 2001 before us today offers immediate help. It is big enough to make a difference in a $10 trillion economy. It is focused on improving incentives to work and invest. And it is effective now."

From an economic point of view, this was misleading. Calling the bill a stimulus package made even less economic sense when one considered its most loudly touted provision: lowering individual tax rates more quickly than the law passed in June 2001 had mandated.

Speeding up the cuts in individual income tax rates may have sounded like a surefire economic stimulus, but the White House's own arguments in favor of the original tax cut law undermined that notion. In lobbying for a ten-year stretch of tax cuts that was likely to become permanent, President Bush and the neoconomists had emphasized the importance of permanent changes. Temporary changes in tax rates, they argued, would not lead people to change their behavior.* As R. Glenn Hubbard said on May 23, 2001, "Permanent cuts in marginal tax rates will have immediate and significant economic effects. Indeed, the evidence is that a purely temporary 'stimulus' tax change would have much more modest impacts than the President's plan."

Yet speeding up the planned tax cuts would supply just that: a temporary change. According to the 2001 law, the individual income tax rates were scheduled to hit bottom in 2006. Accelerating the cuts would therefore make no difference in tax rates from 2006 forward. Whatever reaction consumers and businesses had to those cuts would not change, either. The only new thing would be lower rates in the earlier years, offering just a short window of unexpectedly higher after-tax incomes.

It was a one-time thing, not a permanent or recurring change. By the neoconomists' own logic, households would spread the bonus out into the future,

* As in the scenarios of the $100,000 lottery prize in Chapter 4.

making few changes to their spending in the next couple of years. The economic stimulus would be weak indeed.

Unconvinced by the motives, methods and timing of the House's proposal, the Democratic-controlled Senate sat on it for months. In December, the House passed another package that was little changed from the first; this one dropped the repeal of the corporate alternative minimum tax and included some extra money for state welfare systems. It, too, hit the Senate floor like a lead balloon. Finally, in February 2002, the Senate passed a bill whose main purpose was to extend the unemployment insurance available to the roughly 4 million people who were receiving benefits through the state systems.* In order to move it to the White House's desk, though, the senators would have to negotiate with their colleagues in the House.

By the time the two sides reached agreement, three weeks later, almost all of the tax-cutting provisions had been removed. This didn't occur because the senators wanted to fend off the neoconomy, or at least they never said so. They just didn't buy the idea that all those tax cuts were really necessary or appropriate. The unemployment benefits would be extended, and areas victimized by the terror attacks would receive some new aid. But the only boons to businesses and investors were

---

* Those people represented only about half, depending on how one adjusts the figures for seasonal changes, of the more than 8 million Americans looking for a job that month.

changes in rules for depreciation and the allocation of losses to different tax years. The Congressional Budget Office and the Joint Committee on Taxation estimated that the whole bill would cost just $124 billion over the coming three years. That sum was a little more than half of what Mr. Thomas's version would have cost. It would raise economic growth by a maximum of 0.4 percent a year, but only assuming that all the givebacks were spent and not saved—an unlikely turn of events.

The budget office asserted that the economy would grow a little faster, eventually leading to slightly higher tax revenues. During the ten-year window it used for measuring budget surpluses, the bill would therefore cost just $42 billion. And the title of the bill had changed, too, by the time it reached the president's desk. To fit the mood of the times, it had become the Job Creation and Worker Assistance Act of 2002. Of course, given the size of its provisions, no one expected the new law to create very many jobs.

It was the neoconomists' first major reverse. They had lost a skirmish, but the revolution was far from over. Indeed, it had just begun.

If a stronger economy materialized, it would soon refill the Treasury's coffers. Within a few years, the neoconomists might indeed have been able to claim that the federal government could afford a new tax cut, another step towards the neoconomy.

Could they wait that long? Patience is always hard to

come by in politics, given the rigors of the electoral cycle. But the economic cycle makes patience even more difficult, since the labor market is one of the last markets to recover.

The reason has to do with employers' decision-making. It's hard to forecast how long economic weakness will last, so companies usually slim down their workforces whenever demand for their products and services drops. They typically wait until it's clear that the economy will be in a slump for a while, then carefully trim away unneeded positions. The biggest companies often hire outside consultants to recommend areas for job cuts.

This process takes time. After the previous recession had ended, in March 1991, the unemployment rate didn't reach its peak for another 15 months. No company wants to be caught short-handed when the economy's vigor returns, of course, but even the nation's top economists usually can't decide when a revival began until many months after the fact.

Even though the economy was expected to grow faster in 2002, as the full effects of the Federal Reserve's interest rate cuts pervaded financial markets, the ranks of jobless Americans were likely to grow for several months. Faced with a higher unemployment rate in the midst of quickening economic growth, the White House had two choices: either counsel patience, on the theory that jobs would soon follow growth, or try to give the economy another shot in the arm.

President Bush chose a combination in his second budget proposal, which he delivered to Congress in February 2002. He called on Congress to do much of what the House had already agreed to do: speed up the tax cuts for individuals, reform the alternative minimum tax on businesses and offer more benefits to unemployed Americans. But in addition, in a possible concession to the budget hawks, he proposed slowing down the growth of the federal government's spending and balancing its budget by 2005. Cutting spending could actually hurt the economy in the short term, according to logic that had been unquestioned since Keynes's time.* Yet those two goals, along with the tax changes, were listed under "Returning to Economic Vitality." It suggested that perhaps, after all, some in the Bush administration recognized that deficits could hurt the economy.

Clearly, yet another shift in rhetoric was required to make sure the White House's agenda kept pace with economic reality. So far, however, it looked like the neoconomists still hadn't found a politically attractive rationale for keeping their vision alive.

As the summer of 2002 approached, the debate about the economy shifted from Washington to Wall Street. Many forecasters there were expecting the economy to grow rapidly in the second half of the year. For the opti-

---

* Repealing some of the tax cuts would have the same effects, at least directionally, on the budget and the economy. But this clearly wasn't an option.

mists, the focus was on the manufacturing sector, which was operating at just 73 percent of capacity after slowing down for six straight quarters. By the time the summer came, these economists said, the cocktail for recovery in the sector would be a potent one. Manufacturers would have cleared out all their extra inventory. At the same time, with interest rates at all-time lows and the threat of terror apparently fading, consumers—the economy's main support—would turn on the spending taps. Much of that unused capacity would soon go to work, and then businesses, too, could join in the spending spree. The economy, these forecasters said, was ready to break its chains.

At the same time, a devoted brigade of pessimists predicted another recession—a "double dip." They argued that households and companies would be crushed under a truckload of debt as soon as the economy began to recover, engendering a new crash. The debt was indeed substantial. Households' overall debts were at their highest level since the mid-1980's: about 14 percent of after-tax income, on average. Since the early 1990's, virtually all of the increase in debts had come from consumer credit—borrowing that did not include mortgages—which had doubled from 1994 to 2002.

Because of the low interest rates engendered by the Fed's actions, the debt burden did not present an immediate cause for alarm. Though the debts may have looked huge in comparison to households' income, the debt service—the payments they had to make to stay afloat—was still manageable. The danger, of course, was that interest rates would suddenly rise, making those debts untenable. If interest rates rose because of a reinvigoration of the economy, then the better times might also help consumers to pay off their debts, and catastrophe might be avoided. But if they rose for another reason, say the rapid worsening of the federal government's own bottom line, then consumers might be headed for disaster. Bankruptcies, foreclosures and a lightning-fast tightening of credit markets by snake-bitten lenders would likely push the economy into another recession.

Awareness of the danger, of course, was the first step to avoiding it. Given the possible harm to the economy, it seemed likely that the Fed, and lenders too, would do everything possible to stave off an implosion of the consumer credit markets. Businesses, however, were already having a much tougher time borrowing because of the uncertainty in the economic outlook and the ongoing rash of corporate scandals. Markets for short-term corporate loans like commercial paper were drying up, and companies trying to lock in low long-term interest rates with bond issues were undergoing closer scrutiny.

The doomsayers garnered some credibility as the economy hit another speed bump in the second quarter of 2002. After growing by 5 percent in the first quarter—a rate high enough, if sustained, to create new jobs—the economy only expanded by 1.3 percent in the next three months. Workers' productivity grew by 1 percent. If the same workforce could produce 1 percent more stuff, but the economy only needed 1.3 percent more stuff, not many unemployed people would find jobs. Over time, under these conditions, population growth reflected in the size of the workforce would push up the unemployment rate. Still, the consensus among forecasters was that the growth trend would tick upwards again in the second half of the year.

Another threat to poison the expected recovery was brewing elsewhere, however, and this one would prove to be more damaging. With the American economy on the back burner, President Bush had turned his energies and attentions to a country 6,000 miles away: Iraq.

There may well have been economic reasons for attacking Iraq. Many critics of the administration, as they had during the first Gulf War, suspected that important unstated reasons for war were to pry open some of the world's biggest reserves of oil and natural gas, and to give business to military contractors close to the Bush administration. A stated reason, though less emphasized than the apparently misguided talk of weapons of mass destruction and Iraq's links to Al Qaeda, was to create a cascade of democracy in the Middle East that would potentially weaken terrorist threats to the Western world. There was clearly an economic benefit to be reaped here: with terror minimized, American businesses would carry slightly less risk. All other things equal, their stock prices would rise, their cost of credit would fall, and they would not have to pay quite so much for security and insurance on their buildings and operations. At least, that's the way the argument could have gone.

In the summer of 2002, however, the public did not yet see war as a sure thing.* The Bush administration was just beginning to rattle its saber at the United Nations. And in that state of relative calm, the economy did manage a return to rapid growth: 4 percent in the third quarter of the year—a level economists generally regarded as high enough to generate new jobs.

The year had begun with a streak of seven straight months of job losses, for a total of 457,000 positions— equivalent to the entire working-age population of South Dakota. But the jobs did arrive, right on schedule with the faster economic growth. The nation's payrolls grew by 184,000 from August through October, on a pace to erase almost all the earlier losses by the year's end.

Had the economy managed to steer clear of more shocks, through the fall and the holiday shopping season, then that rosy outcome may indeed have come to pass. By November, however, the drumbeat for war was unmistakable. In September, the White House had released its new National Security Strategy, allowing for pre-emptive strikes against other countries. In October, Congress authorized the use of force in Iraq. The prob-

---

* War with Iraq may have been a sure thing much earlier from the White House's point of view, according to revelations in early 2004 from former members of the Bush administration.

lem was that no one knew exactly when war would come or how much it would cost.

In the post–9/11 world, the costs of war could have added up to much more than another hole in the federal government's budget. An attack on a Muslim country in the Middle East threatened to unleash another wave of terrorism, according to some pundits. The Florence Fund, a non-profit lobbying group, even ran a full-page advertisement in *The New York Times,* with Osama bin Laden striking an Uncle Sam-like pose and saying, "I Want You to Invade Iraq." More terror in the United States—experts at the time especially feared a missile strike on a passenger plane, as had been attempted in November in Kenya—could cripple the transport industry and dampen spending by businesses and consumers across all sectors.

Prognosticators also worried that Saddam Hussein's regime would engage in acts of terror, perhaps bombing oil fields in his own country or neighboring Saudi Arabia in order to damage the world's wealthy economies. The price of crude oil dipped briefly in November, when a diplomatic solution to the question of Iraqi arms seemed possible. But when no progress occurred, the oil price began to rise again, shooting from about $25 a barrel to more than $32 by the end of the year. A conflagration in the Gulf could hurt the supply of the black stuff in several ways, depending on how oil-rich nations reacted to it, and could exact a severe toll from the economy. Families were already paying bigger bills for heating oil and gasoline; companies had to pay more for transportation, both for their products and their people.

The most pervasive problem, however, was uncertainty. The timing and character of the war were hard to predict. Business forecasters became akin to military tacticians as they tried to anticipate when an attack would occur, how long it would take and how intense the fighting might be. Would victory occur within weeks, or would Saddam Hussein manage to draw the United States into a prolonged, bloody struggle?

The outcome in economic terms was just as hard to guess; the range of possibilities was tremendous. A study headed up by Laurence H. Meyer, a former governor of the Federal Reserve, suggested that a quick, successful war might help the economy by as much as $52 billion, assuming the victory emboldened consumers. But the same study stated that in the worst case, a vicious conflict might cost the economy $472 billion in 2002 alone—about the same effect as closing down the entire state of Illinois for a year.

Whatever the eventual outcome of the war itself, the uncertainty leading up to it had immediate effects. Economic activity slowed palpably in the fourth quarter of 2002, and companies again began shedding jobs. Though retail sales were reasonably strong during the holiday shopping season, many analysts judged it a disappointment. Economic growth eventually clocked in at just 1.4 percent—another lousy quarter—as a familiar pall crept back over a beleaguered nation.

*

With the resumption of job losses and a lack of momentum for a new stimulus bill, the White House desperately needed to energize its economic agenda. The method it chose was housecleaning. On Friday, December 6, without any warning, the president handed Paul H. O'Neill, the Treasury secretary, and Lawrence B. Lindsey, his top economic adviser, their hats. The two men had been told only the previous evening that their services would no longer be needed.

In its first two years, the Bush administration had refused, nearly uniformly, to admit any mistakes on any decision or issue. That self-projected aura of infallibility would be damaged by sacking any of its own hires. Yet pundits had been whispering for months that if anyone suffered the axe at the midpoint of President Bush's term, it would be Mr. O'Neill.

From outside the capital, the Treasury secretary seemed like a maverick who had never succeeded in cracking the inner circles of power in Washington, whether in Congress or in the White House. Paradoxically, despite his vaunted position, there was little reason to blame him for the continued weakness of the economy. Despite the early unanimity among the Bush team, Mr. O'Neill had been skeptical of the necessity of big new tax cuts, except in the case of corporate profits. And he had what in Washington was a fatal flaw: he spoke his mind, whatever happened to be on it. The problem was so acute that *The Economist* dubbed him "tongue on the loose" only a few months into his tenure. Some of his more memorable one-liners included:

> We are not pursuing, as often said, a policy of a strong dollar.
>
> (The dollar dropped 1.5% against the euro after this comment.)
>
> February 16, 2001

> Part of what you saw on Friday last week was show business. . . . By my reckoning, what they did is more than we'd like.
>
> (On the House's Economic Security and Recovery Act)
>
> October 15, 2001

> Companies come and go. It's . . . part of the genius of capitalism.
>
> (On Enron's collapse)
>
> January 13, 2002

As a result of Mr. O'Neill's skepticism and unique brand of bluntness, it seemed, the main levers of economic policy had been taken out of his hands for much of his time as treasury secretary. His own initiatives were mostly confined to the international sphere, dealing with issues like financing for terrorism, poor countries' indebtedness and the financial crisis in Argentina.

Elaine L. Chao, the labor secretary, also appeared to have little say in the nation's economic policy. But she had mastered the Washingtonian art of saying a lot while saying surprisingly little. The worst she could be accused of was declaring, in an interview on June 7, 2002, that "the recovery is here."* She may not have had much power, but she kept her job.

The power to shape the nation's future certainly did rest with Messrs Hubbard and Lindsey, the true neoconomists. Their hallmarks were clearly stamped on the policies put forward by the White House and the Republican leadership in the House of Representatives. But despite their similarities in ideology, each man's standing within the administration had developed in a vastly different way. Mr. Lindsey had raised President Bush's ire, according to reports at the time of his resignation, for suggesting in September 2002 that a war in Iraq might cost as much as $200 billion. The figure had seemed astronomical at the time, and naming it had not helped the cause of the neocons on the foreign policy side. Mr. Lindsey also appeared to have made few close allies in Congress.

Professor Hubbard, by contrast, had cultivated the image of the cool, deeply knowledgeable mastermind of the Bush administration's economic policy. In his speeches he relied more on substance than did Mr. Lind-

---

* I interviewed Ms. Chao several times and never came back with anything controversial or newsworthy. A better reporter might have extracted something juicy, but I doubt it.

sey, who was given to rhetorical flourish. In his testimony before Congress he was virtually impossible to fluster.

Where Professor Hubbard appeared to be a solid asset, Mr. Lindsey was tending towards a liability. This divergence suited the administration's purposes well. It needed a fall guy—and not just Mr. O'Neill, who could barely take credit or blame for the state of the economy. But a complete housecleaning would have signaled a repudiation of the economic policies of the past two years, something that a prideful President Bush probably would have found distasteful. The White House needed to create a break with the recent past but, at the same time, stick to its plans without losing face.

Mr. Lindsey, a longtime friend of President Bush, was taken by surprise when the axe fell. But the White House softened the blow by saying—and here was the ingenious bit—that there was nothing wrong with the strategy hatched by Mr. Lindsey and Professor Hubbard; it just needed new salesmen to convince the American people of its correctness.

Professor Hubbard kept his position, for reasons that would soon become apparent. But rumors of his return to New York were starting to make the rounds. They were logical inferences, given that his leave of absence from Columbia's Graduate School of Business was only slated to last two years. He told the White House that he could extend the leave, though he showed only moderate eagerness to remain in Washington. Within a couple of months, he left Washington of his own accord.

*

With the departures of Messrs Lindsey and O'Neill, George W. Bush could choose reliable keepers for the neoconomy's flame. So whom would he bring to Washington, as salesmen for a policy that had already been decided?

To replace the wayward Mr. O'Neill, President Bush chose a true believer. Just hours after Mr. O'Neill handed in his resignation, President Bush called John W. Snow, chief executive of CSX, a major rail freight company, to offer him the job of Treasury secretary. He was another alumnus of Gerald Ford's administration, like Richard B. Cheney (the vice president), Donald H. Rumsfeld (the defense secretary) and Mr. O'Neill. But unlike Mr. O'Neill, he seemed to have more of the other two men's political savvy. And, as it would soon become clear, he was committed to the basic tenets of the neoconomists' strategy: lower taxes, more saving and more capital.

On the following Thursday, the White House announced that Stephen Friedman would succeed Mr. Lindsey. At the time of his selection, Mr. Friedman was co-chairman of Goldman Sachs, one of the Wall Street firms that had come to be known in the press as "financial services giants" because of their involvement in almost every aspect of matters relating to money.

Though the White House said he would be a salesman for its existing economic plan, Mr. Friedman's selection still represented something of a departure for the Bush administration. For one thing, Mr. Friedman was a board member of the Concord Coalition, an organization advocating budget discipline that had sharply criticized the corporate bonuses in the latest economic legislation. As recently as August 2002, the coalition's president had strongly warned against any more ambitious tax cuts or spending plans.

But perhaps more importantly, Mr. Bush had scrupulously avoided picking a Wall Street insider for any top economic post at the beginning of his term. The White House wanted to send the message, it seemed, that economic policy would not be determined by financiers in New York. This stance struck a contrast with President Clinton's last two treasury secretaries, Robert E. Rubin and his protégé, Lawrence H. Summers. Both of them had become well-known for counseling in private with the big Wall Street firms, the International Monetary Fund and the Federal Reserve as the world's financial markets weathered a succession of crises in the 1990's.

The Bush administration and its Republican allies in Congress had been trying for some time to differentiate their own policies from "Rubinomics," an ill-defined term said to denote the piecemeal economic policy of the Clinton administration. It's not clear exactly why they wanted to do this, given the record-setting boom Mr. Clinton presided over in the 1990's. Perhaps the White House wanted to distance itself from a perception that the concerns of other nations, or their agents, played some part in American economic policy. More likely, the White House was trying to tar the Clinton administration for causing the bubble in the stock market. Or maybe the White House just needed an enemy.

In any case, Mr. Rubin's name was effectively mud in Republican circles in 2002. How strange, then, that Mr.

Friedman was arriving from the very same post that Mr. Rubin had held at the very same firm, Goldman Sachs, until 1992. What was to be the payoff from the bizarre turnaround in the White House's staffing philosophy?

For one thing, Mr. Friedman did not kick off his tenure with any of Mr. Lindsey's bluster or Mr. O'Neill's gaffes. In fact, he remained virtually invisible until his first public appearance, at the Federal Reserve Bank of New York, in February 2003. But by then, the neoconomists had already launched the second big step in their peaceful revolution.

9

THE NEOCONOMY VICTORIOUS

The first duty of a revolutionary is to get away with it.
—ABBIE HOFFMAN

Revolutions don't always go smoothly from start to finish, as the neoconomists found out in 2002. Just as the American Revolution had jolted from the early excitement of successful guerrilla raids to the bloody reality of costly defeats on land and sea, the neoconomists had watched the seemingly irresistible momentum of their big tax cut disappear amid the dust and soot of terror, scandal, deficits and joblessness.

But like the dogged colonials, the neoconomists soldiered on. With reinforcements installed at the White House and Treasury, they were ready to fight in 2003. Victory would come again, and so would plans for many more.

A new tax cut was on the way, one that would be even more skewed towards the neoconomists' ultimate goal than the first one. In addition, they would introduce a weapon that could speed the revolution towards its conclusion like none before: a vast expansion of tax-free saving accounts. And before the year was out, they would reveal plans to make their tax cuts permanent, as well as an initiative that would put the government's biggest program at the service of the neoconomy.

But let's not get ahead of ourselves. Before any of this could happen, the Bush administration had to dig its economic policy out of a very deep rut.

*   *   *

On the eve of 2003, the neoconomists had little to show for their efforts. It wasn't really surprising, of course. The realization of the neoconomy was supposed to take place years into the future, and the policies designed to achieve it were not meant to transform the present. Yet the politically irritating fact remained: neither the economy nor the labor market was making a solid recovery.

From an economic perspective, the lack of a spark was not surprising. The wave of shocks the nation had suffered—the bursting of the stock market bubble, the 9/11 terror attacks, corporate scandals and uncertainty about the war in Iraq—would have left any economy feeling sluggish. Moreover, the core of the neoconomists' strategy had targeted long-term, not short-term, improvements in economic growth. Until corporate profits rose perceptibly, there was no reason to expect any signs of life in the labor market.

Nonetheless, the labor market had become a constant thorn in the Bush administration's side. The Labor

Department had recorded a thinning of the nation's payrolls in 18 out of the 24 months of George W. Bush's presidency. The department's statisticians always announced their figures at 8:30 A.M. Eastern Time on the first Friday of the month. On 18 of those 24 Fridays, the White House was left playing defense for the rest of the day, and sometimes throughout the weekend.

The neoconomists might have gained some more sympathy from the press and public if they had pursued an economic policy more narrowly focused on a short-term expansion of demand. This kind of strategy wouldn't necessarily imply a Roosevelt-style New Deal, with the federal government itself stepping in to employ or subsidize the employment of millions of jobless Americans; that sort of extreme response seemed out of proportion to what had been, in terms of economic activity, a fairly mild recession. But economists of all types—academics, think tankers, Wall Streeters and government staffers—did criticize the administration for failing to aim more of the 2001 tax cuts at working-class people. As research had showed, working-class Americans would have been more likely to spend the money rather than save it. The resulting surge in spending might have lifted the economy out of its slump.

But telling the neoconomists to focus on the short term was like asking the proverbial leopard to do something about those little dark blotches in its fur. The neoconomists wanted the government to take less of people's money, but mostly so a substantial share of that money could be funneled into the corporate sector and spent on new capital. Thus they aimed their tax cuts at the wealthy. These were the people, after all, who would save the biggest share of whatever money was returned to them.

*   *   *

In Washington, disagreements about the conduct of economic policy took center stage, as Democrats exploited what had become the Bush administration's main vulnerability. There was little the administration could do; until more jobs appeared, they had to resign themselves to an almost monthly hammering.

Even looking forward, the administration was facing a political predicament. If a strong recovery finally did come, as many forecasters predicted for the second half of 2003, it might end up being too distant from the first big wave of tax cuts for George W. Bush to take all the credit. The president would have to admit that his policies really had long-term, or at least medium-term, goals all along. And the Federal Reserve, which had cut short-term interest rates again in November 2002, could just as easily claim the laurels; after all, its moves rarely affected the economy immediately.

Or, perhaps more likely, the discerning public would chalk up the recovery to the economy's natural cycle. Indeed, policy was not the only thing holding the economy back. In the job market, other important factors were also at work.

The productivity of the labor force—the amount of goods and services they could produce within a fixed period of time—had risen by an astonishing 8.3 percent in the fourth quarter of 2001, and followed that performance with a still-more-amazing 9.3 percent in the first three months of 2002. When the workers who already had jobs became more productive so rapidly, it wasn't hard to figure out why companies didn't need to hire more. The demand for American goods and services, both at home and abroad, had only grown by 2.7 and 5 percent in those quarters—nowhere near enough to keep up with the gains in productivity. It was becoming a familiar refrain: businesses could let even more workers go and still satisfy the demand for stuff to buy. And that's just what they did.

Some of the sources of productivity did have their limits. After a year or two, the more painful ones—those of the working-fingers-to-the-bone-for-the-same-pay variety—were likely to disappear, as some people searched for and found less arduous jobs. And while workers may have been willing to meet higher expectations in a job market that seemed temporarily lousy, they might not have looked kindly on managers who expected 110 percent even after the economy returned to normalcy. Still, neither workers nor managers would forget the practices that helped them to become more productive when times were tough.

Another reason why companies could easily justify putting off hiring was the rising cost of the workers themselves. Wages and salaries had grown by about 7 percent, in total, during 2001 and 2002. Meanwhile, prices for the goods and services companies produced rose by just 4 percent. This difference might not have been a problem for businesses, since their workers were also becoming more productive. But during the same two years, the cost of employee benefits had grown by more than 10 percent, and it was still accelerating.

Health insurance companies, facing higher prices for medical care, were starting to look for ways to charge more for coverage. They could pass a certain amount straight to workers in employer-provided health plans by raising deductibles and co-payments. In many plans, doctors' visits or prescriptions that used to cost $5 or $10 now cost $15 or $20.

Insurers were raising premiums, too. Employers usu- ally paid the bulk of insurance premiums, since they could do so using before-tax dollars (unlike employees). Even so, the extra burden of higher premiums would be shared between employers and employees; to compen- sate for the higher premiums, employers could slow down increases in wages or raise the share of the premi- ums paid by workers. They could also cut the cost of benefits by offering less generous health plans. But these changes might have angered workers. The alterna- tive was just to hire fewer.

Pension funds, still hurting from the deep dip in the stock market, were also putting a squeeze on businesses. A few had held as much as 90 percent of their money in stocks—hardly something a conservative investor would do. Others, especially those controlled in part by employ- ees, had kept large portions of their assets in their own stock rather than diversifying risks using the market.

Companies of all sizes and stripes found that their portfolios were no longer earning enough to make the payments they had pledged to their retirees. The only way to keep their promises was to top up their pension funds with profits or borrowing. Even at the end of 2001, pension experts forecast that the shortfalls' effects on corporate balance sheets would be felt well into 2003.

Putting the labor market aside, perhaps the most important reason why companies were not eager to hire in early 2003 was what might have been called the 'twice-burned' problem. A year earlier, the forecasters had told them to expect strong growth in the summer and fall, enough to justify bringing in new workers. But the hopes had ended in disappointment when concern about the war in Iraq, perhaps combined with other unrelated factors, curtailed the economy's momentum. With an attack in the Middle East apparently imminent in the first months of 2003, and the results of war so uncertain, executives were loath to bet on an optimistic forecast. Some had expanded their businesses too quickly a year earlier, so a wait-and-see strategy seemed safer this time.

Yet at the same time, the forecasters confidently told of a robust recovery in the second half of the year. In the January edition of the *Wall Street Journal*'s semi-annual survey of economic seers, 35 out of 54 predicted growth at a rate of 3.5 percent or more—almost certainly enough to create jobs—in both the summer and fall.

At this moment, salving the wounds of the jobless

and struggling, nursing them along for another six months, might have made both political and economic sense. The current malaise was expected to give way to better times, but in the meantime Washington could usefully ease people's pain. Conventional economic theory certainly did not recommend a big tax cut, however, just as the economy was regaining its footing. Another set of cuts would barely benefit the jobless, and it might also have spurred the economy enough that the Federal Reserve would have to start worrying about inflation again. If the fire was just starting to blaze, you didn't want to add more lighter fluid.*

So the neoconomists found themselves, once more, in a conundrum. How could they sell the American public, and its representatives in Washington, on another step towards the neoconomy, or perhaps even two? The economy's needs just didn't seem to match up with the neoconomists' vision. Would they finally show their hand, revealing to one and all just what the neoconomy was all about? Well, not quite.

*   *   *

The neoconomists called their newest tax-cutting plan "growth insurance," a term which, in its subtleties, gave away the Bush administration's latest sales strategy. It was a term that Professor Hubbard had equated, a couple of times in the past, to that old chestnut, economic stimulus. But in the battle for hearts and minds, giving

---

* That bottle could blow up in your hand, after all.

"growth insurance" top billing killed three, maybe five birds with one stone.

First and most obviously, the phrase avoided the word "stimulus." That word suited neither the economic forecasts, which had dulled any sense of urgency, nor the long-term goals of the neoconomists' strategy.

Second, the word "insurance" suggested that the neoconomists were proposing something responsible—a sensible safety net in case the economy couldn't right itself; a Plan B that would definitely pay off.

Third, the phrase implied that the forecasts were not enough, by themselves, to justify complacency. In this way, it suited the mood of corporate America to a T. Insurance was what many businesses, especially those that had been burned in 2002, were looking for before they would commit to any expansion of production or payrolls.

Fourth, it did not imply that the White House's previous policies were wrong. You buy insurance to protect against the unpredictable, after you've done everything in your power to make sure things come out okay. The White House had done its best, the term seemed to say, but a little extra security was needed in the unlikely event that those earlier policies didn't work out.

Yet there was something of a contradiction in this line of thinking, given the definition of insurance. Insurance is *guaranteed* to pay off, if only in the event of a catastrophe or loss. If the Bush administration's insurance plan really was a sure-fire recipe for economic growth, guaranteed to work if the slump continued, why hadn't they tried it in the first place? Why wasn't the so-called insurance plan Plan A? And another thing—how had they managed to design a policy that would *not* work if the economy *did* recover?* It didn't quite add up.

Still, fifth, no one could say the White House was doing nothing.

Whether they were doing the right thing was another question. The president's plan, the gist of which had already been leaked in late December, had two main parts. The first was the old saw: speed up all the tax cuts initially scheduled by the June 2001 law. The second, the centerpiece, was completely new: abolish the income tax on dividends from shares.

In total, according to the White House's estimates, the plan would cost $670 billion over ten years. By the time the House of Representatives put their version together, it cost $726 billion.† What the Bush administration stressed, however, was that the plan might create as many as 1.4 million jobs—extra jobs that would not otherwise have appeared—between July 2003 and December 2004.

The White House attributed almost two-thirds of the new jobs to the acceleration of the 2001 tax cuts. From the perspective of accepted economic theory, however,

* Thus neatly avoiding the problem of the exploding bottle of lighter fluid.

† To paraphrase Homer Simpson: mmm, pork. (Actually, Homer said bacon.)

there was reason to be skeptical that a big rise in consumers' spending would result from the acceleration of planned tax cuts. The extra money that made it into Americans' pockets would represent a temporary, not permanent, change.

Dropping the dividend tax—an essential step in the pursuit of the neoconomy—was supposed to account for the other 400,000 to 500,000 new jobs in the 18-month window outlined by the White House, at a cost of about $350 billion. This boost for the labor market was a crucial element in the sales strategy. Most Americans received very little of their income from dividends, so the Bush administration had to find another way to gain the public's support for such an expensive plan.

Yet for a multitude of reasons, the predicted effect on job creation was little more than a guess. The administration argued that if investors no longer had to pay tax on the dividends they received, the value of their shares would increase—as long as the company that sold the shares continued to pay out dividends at the same rate. Other investors would be willing to pay more for the shares, given their higher after-no-tax return. Share prices would rise instantly.

Multiply that effect across the whole market. Suddenly, millions upon millions of shares are worth more. Investors feel wealthier, and they begin to spend more money. Businesses, their share prices back up from post-bubble lows, find that they can buy up other businesses more easily. The economy hums with excitement, and soon there are jobs aplenty.

That's what the White House said would happen. And there were companies—including Microsoft, one of the nation's most cash-rich businesses—that declared dividends for the first time in anticipation of the legislation. With one tax on their profits removed, they decided more of the cash belonged in investors' hands.

But this reaction wouldn't necessarily become the norm. There was a chance that companies would actually lower their dividends in response to the legislation. Economists have struggled for years to figure out why companies pay any dividends at all, rather than simply keeping all their profits to invest in new projects. One explanation is to send a signal of success to investors. Another is that dividends make stocks more attractive to certain kinds of investors—often referred to generically as "widows and orphans"—who rely on fixed incomes from their portfolios. Without a personal tax on dividends, companies would find that they could send the same signal or offer the same fixed income by *lowering* their payouts. If a dividend of $1 had been taxed at 28 percent, then the investor was left with $0.72. With no tax, the company could simply pay out $0.72, or a slightly higher figure, and keep the rest.*

If companies behaved in this way, their share prices might rise only modestly in response to the legislation; it would depend on how investors rated the new projects

---

* Companies already paid out money tax-free by repurchasing shares from their owners. However, if these repurchases appeared to become routine, the Internal Revenue Service would consider them dividends and tax them.

the companies would finance with the extra money left over. If a company's executives decided to use that cash to buy a private jet with gold-plated fixtures and a golf ball cleaner, its stock price might even drop.

No one could say for sure which would predominate: higher dividends, or lower. Finding out would take time, since companies almost never lowered their dividends. That was the worst sort of signal—what, you can't pay anymore? Much preferred was simply to keep the dividend steady, in dollar terms, over time as the share price increased.

Even if more money did make it into the hands of taxpayers, it was not certain that they would spend it. It was peculiar that the neoconomists, whose plan was conceived to encourage saving in the long term, were touting its ability to encourage spending in the short term. In the event, that spending was unlikely to amount to much, since dividend income flowed mostly to the wealthiest Americans—they were among the least likely to spend extra income rather than saving it. Moreover, the anticipated rocketing of the stock market would be a one-time event, not an annual tradition, and economic theory predicted that its effects on income and wealth would be spread over many years.

For someone struggling to find a job in the first months of 2003, these concerns were probably the most important. But for economists more interested in the nation's long-term living standards and its capacity to produce, the potential for immediate stimulus was overshadowed by the faint outline of an elephant in the room. To them, the tax on dividends created a special kind of economic problem. They saw that the main effect of removing it was likely to be ephemeral, but huge. The change would eliminate inefficiencies that had dogged the nation's financial markets for decades, costing companies and investors countless opportunities to do business.

It all came down to the way companies raised money to finance new projects. In basic terms, they had two options: sell equity—that is, shares in the company's assets and profits—or borrow. Each option came with different strings attached. Borrowing meant paying interest according to fixed rules; selling equity gave the company's managers discretion to pay dividends as they wished. Unpaid debts could send the company into bankruptcy, forcing its board and executives to surrender control to creditors; selling shares usually meant giving up control bit by bit.

There were many reasons why companies might choose to borrow rather than sell shares, or vice-versa. Perhaps they signaled something about their own prospects for profitability by choosing one route or the other. Economists had been arguing this question for years. But they almost always agreed that the tax system was a factor that companies couldn't ignore. The reason was simple: the federal government *did* tax corporate income used to pay dividends but *did not* tax corporate income used to pay interest on debts.

This part of the tax system was one of the biggest thorns in economists' sides. The dividend tax discouraged selling shares and encouraged borrowing, though it was unclear why this was in society's best interest. According to economic theory, removing the tax would increase the amount of financing available to businesses and raise returns. Without the government driving a wedge between returns to stocks and bonds, more companies and investors would be able to choose the financing options that suited them best.

The simplest option for removing the double taxation of dividends was to allow companies to deduct dividends they paid from their taxable profits. This way, only individuals would owe taxes on earnings paid out as dividends and interest, with the same rate for both.* The money companies earned had to go to people, eventually. Wouldn't it have been simpler just to tax the people, instead?

Perhaps. But since late 2001, the hit machine known as the corporate sector had brought the American public such smashes as Enron, Global Crossing and WorldCom. So how would the news go down that the very same corporate sector would no longer have to pay a dime in tax?

Whatever the answer, it was enough to give even the neoconomists in Washington second thoughts. So they took a different approach. Rather than leveling the play-

---

* The government could have achieved the same result by making interest paid on debts subject to the corporate income tax. Such a move would not have been in keeping with the White House's economic policies, to say the least. It would also have created new distortions, though even expert economists could not predict exactly how big or where.

ing field for shares by taking away the tax on the corporate side, they would take it away on the individual side.

Born of political expediency, this solution was a clumsy one. Americans with the highest incomes, in the top tax bracket, would pay a rate of 35 percent on dividends and interest after the 2001 tax cuts came into full effect in 2006. The corporate income tax rate, at least for businesses making the big money, was 35 percent. So exempting dividends from the personal income tax looked like it just might possibly have the same effect as exempting them from the corporate income tax.

The reality was a little different, as anyone familiar with the complexity of America's tax system and financial markets could easily have guessed. Though the people with the highest incomes certainly owned more shares than their working-class counterparts, private investors did not own all shares directly. A significant portion of the nation's publicly traded shares, perhaps as much as a third according to an estimate from the AFL-CIO, were owned by pension funds. When pension funds paid benefits using the dividends from the shares they owned, the money often counted as ordinary income for the retirees who received it. In other words, it was taxable.

In addition, not all dividends would receive the special treatment. Strangely, dividends paid by companies that did not pay federal income tax—either because they did not earn profits or because they found enough loopholes to erase their obligations—would still be subject to personal income tax. Dividends paid by preferred stock, which typically gives investors a stronger claim on a company's assets than does common stock, would also miss out on tax-free status.

There were other wrinkles, too, but they didn't seem to matter to the Bush administration. They had found a politically acceptable way to win one of the great battles in the pursuit of the neoconomy: unshackling Americans' shares in the capital of the nation's public and private companies from the yoke of taxation.

*   *   *

Ending double taxation thus became the second plank in the neoconomists' latest platform. It was a cause that George W. Bush would have no trouble fighting for. Just as "growth insurance" sounded wise and prudent, "double taxation" sounded unfair and reprehensible—the sort of thing Patrick Henry might have railed against.

It was also commonplace. In fact, the treatment of corporate income was hardly the tax system's worst offense of this kind. Buying a bottle of beer with your dinner at a restaurant could subject you to taxation *eight* times over, between the taxes on the income you used to buy it (up to four: federal, state and local income taxes, and Social Security's payroll tax), the federal and state governments' excise taxes on the beer itself, and the sales tax (state and possibly local) added to your bill.

Why, buying a beer was a model of injustice! The tax system was an octopus reaching, with every tentacle, into the American wallet! And, oh yes, it also unfairly distorted consumers' choice of beverages, in favor of drinks like orange juice and tea!

Perhaps it was not astonishing that this sort of octuple taxation did not make the headlines, even if it affected many more people than the dividend tax did. Of course, getting rid of excise taxes on beer would not have done much to bring the neoconomy closer, either.

Not that it would have mattered, in terms of what the neoconomists and the rest of the Bush team said in public. No one mentioned just how much closer eliminating taxes on dividends would bring them to the objective of making all saving tax-free. In 2001, dividends made up 12 percent of the capital-related income that taxpayers declared on their returns. Making this income tax-free was a major step forward. But the Bush administration didn't mark this milestone in so many words. Once again, a policy with long-term goals was couched mostly in the language of short-term expectations.

*   *   *

A few weeks after the substance of the latest tax-cutting proposal became public, the Congressional Budget Office released its latest estimates for budget surpluses in the next decade. Just $20 billion, about one-third of one percent of the original total for 2002 through 2011, was left. Deficits would last through 2006, and then the federal government would start to run small surpluses again. But if any more tax cuts became law, including the ones proposed two weeks earlier, most of those surpluses would disappear.

As his initial plans made clear, George W. Bush had intended to find a use for an entire decade's worth of surpluses, even though his own term in office might last only four years. By using the anticipated surpluses up before they could even be collected, the Bush team could grab all the resources of a future administration for itself. The grab would help to fund the first steps in the revolutionary pursuit of the neoconomy, as well allowing George W. Bush to keep costly campaign promises. But now, by backing the House's plan for $726 billion in tax cuts, he was planning to leave his successors not just without wiggle-room but with the burden of heavy deficits, too.

There may have been a method to what many Democrats immediately called fiscal madness. So far, the White House had two reasons for incurring deficits with a raft of new tax cuts. The public reason was to cement an economic recovery. The more fundamental, less discussed reason was to encourage more saving and build a bigger capital stock, bringing the neoconomy still closer. But there was a third reason, this time a political one: to handcuff his successor.

If Democrats won back the White House in 2004, or even 2008, their hands would be tied. Forced to deal with deficits themselves after complaining of George W. Bush's fiscal profligacy, they would be hard-pressed to spend money on the social programs that typically made up their political platform and guaranteed their support from voters. They might even have to raise taxes just to avoid *cutting* spending. And that would open up one of

Republicans' favorite avenues of attack: that Democrats were a bunch of big-government-loving, taxing-and-spending liberals. The real problem, of course, would be that George W. Bush had spent all of the Democrats' money for them. Even if they did win in 2004, the fiscal terrain would be such a minefield that the Republicans would have an easy victory the next time around.

This strategy had been tried before, and it had worked. Ronald Reagan had cast the federal government into deep deficits with a combination of big tax cuts and heavy spending on the military. The only problem was that his successor was not a Democrat, but his own vice president, George H. W. Bush.

This time, the strategy came with a different type of problem. If a Democratic president was forced to raise taxes, he (or Hillary) might be tempted to dismantle what existed of the neoconomy. But this risk didn't seem to bother the neoconomists or the ever-confident George W. Bush.

Part of the reason may have been that 2011 was no longer the end of their time horizon. Two years after taking office, their ten-year window for planning tax cuts had shifted, to 2004–2013. In 2012 and 2013, according to the budget office, the federal government would probably move back into the black—about $1 trillion into the black. This was just the encouragement the neoconomists needed. At a stroke, the United States was no longer a nation with $20 billion in budget surpluses that could ill afford another tax cut, but a nation with $1 trillion in budget surpluses that was ready to step up to the plate—all from shifting the window by just two years.

Naturally, these rose-colored figures could be deceptive. The budget office's estimates did not include the effects of costly new programs, most notably the prescription drug benefit for Medicare—something the president had promised to enact during his campaign. They did not include the cost of a war in Iraq, either. And they certainly did not include anything that an administration elected in 2008 or 2012 might want to spend money on. Bad news for Jeb Bush, perhaps.

More worrying, though, was the notion that what just might happen in 2012 and 2013 could justify what would happen in 2003. Even the cleverest and most confident economists would be hard-pressed to bet their careers on their forecasts for years 9 and 10. Each year further into the future is more difficult to predict than the last. One way to understand why is to imagine yourself taking a walk in an unfamiliar city. You're much more likely to get lost if you have a long way to go than if you only have to walk a few blocks. Moreover, each mistake you make along the way can take you further and further from your ideal route. In essence, the effect of your mistakes multiplies as you make more. The same is true for economic forecasting.

*   *   *

This didn't seem to deter the neoconomists. With the ink barely dry on the latest tax-cutting plan, they proposed a huge step that would bring the neoconomy not just closer, but straight into the homes of most Americans. They were finally tying their colors to the mast. There was no consideration of deficits or stimulus here. The pursuit of the neoconomy was the only possible explanation. It was a mammoth initiative, announced by the Treasury, that no one dared to put a price on: an expansion of tax-free savings accounts so large that it would cover all the investment income of most American families.

They proposed two new kinds of accounts to replace the majority of all accounts that had come before. The first—the Retirement Savings Account—was basically an expanded Roth Individual Retirement Account (Roth IRA), for which its owner could purchase investments with her after-tax income. The investments would earn their returns free of tax, and would be available for equally tax-free withdrawals at age 58 or in case of death or disability. The second type of account—the Lifetime Savings Account—would work the same way, except that its owner could withdraw from it at any time with no penalty.

Every American would be able to contribute $7,500 to *each* account every year, an amount that would rise with inflation. To get an idea of how enormous a tax shelter this could be, just think about a well-to-do family of four. Mom and Dad each set up two accounts apiece, but they also set up four more accounts: a Lifetime and Retirement Saving Account for each of their kids. Now the entire family, with its eight accounts, can shield $60,000 worth of investments from tax every year. Within five years, they could hold a tax-free port-folio worth $300,000—not a bad college fund!

Understandably, private financial planners were lick-ing their lips. They could help their clients to save thou-sands, maybe millions, by shifting their *existing* investments into these accounts. So would anybody actually bother to save *more*? David A. Wise of Harvard, perhaps the world's foremost expert on retirement sav-ing, was skeptical. "When one thinks, 'Are we going to get a lot more saving out of this?' I just don't know," he said at the time.

Some economists even warned of a drop in saving, because the new accounts would replace so-called tradi-tional IRAs, the Roth IRAs' predecessors. At retirement, the income and withdrawals from traditional IRAs were not tax-free. But they did offer an up-front tax deduc-tion for wages that were contributed. As a result, they were more attractive to workers with lower incomes.

Consider a worker who earns $2,200 a month before taxes, levied at 25 percent in total, and has expenses of $1,500 a month. He puts $200 worth of his pre-tax income into his traditional IRA, pays $500 in tax on the remaining $2,000 of his income and has exactly $1,500 left over for his expenses. He breaks even. Now start again, but take away the traditional IRA. The worker pays tax on all his income, leaving him with $1,650. After he pays his $1,500 in expenses, he has just $150 left over to save each month. Sure, he'll eventually withdraw his savings tax-free, but in the meantime his saving rate has dropped by a quarter.

On a national scale, the saving of low-income people could have taken a severe hit, as their most attractive option for retirement saving gradually disappeared. The Treasury didn't see it that way, though. Its press release asserted that "more low and moderate-income taxpayers will participate" in saving, because they would be able to withdraw money at any time—at least from Lifetime Savings Accounts—rather than having to lock it up as in existing retirement accounts. At any rate, the new plan presented two sets of incentives working in opposite directions for working class people. Which would be more powerful was anyone's guess.

For taxpayers with plenty of money to save, the prospect of all this tax-free saving was clearly a reason to salivate. But the more these taxpayers took advantage of the new accounts, the more it would cost the Treasury in forgone revenue. In view of the nation's deteriorating budget situation, there was reason to be wary. Even if the new accounts did increase saving, the faster growth that might result would be years away. In the meantime, would the federal government be creditworthy?

It might, if you believed a more sinister motive behind this latest brainchild of the neoconomists. Some pundits said the tax-free accounts were actually a ploy to move tax revenue from the future to the present—a second raid on the budgets of future administrations, making it harder still for them to fend off the neoconomy and implement their own programs.

This was how it would work. By barring further contributions to traditional IRAs, with their up-front deductions, the Treasury would immediately be able to collect taxes on more wages. The amount might even be enough to outweigh the revenue lost when investors shifted their existing, taxable portfolios into the new, tax-free savings accounts. Of course, the revenue slated for the future, when the owners of traditional IRAs would withdraw and finally pay tax on their money, would also disappear; withdrawals from the new accounts would all be tax-free. So the government would still pay the piper eventually, but not for several more years. More bad news for Jeb, Hillary or whomever.

But to the neoconomists, it probably didn't matter. The new savings accounts would allow them to make an end-run around all the taxes on dividends, interest and capital gains. If the underlying stocks and bonds were all sheltered, those taxes were effectively meaningless. Everyone except the wealthiest investors would be able to shelter their entire portfolios within a decade or so. And the wealthy would still shelter hundreds of thousands of dollars each. The dream of the neoconomy would become, for many, a reality.

In this case, the Bush administration made no bones about the superficial goal of greater saving. "The two simple accounts will have one powerful goal—making saving for everyday life and retirement security easier and more attractive," said Pamela Olson, the assistant secretary of the Treasury who announced the plan. But there was no explanation of how more saving might affect the economy in the long run. The effect on the neoconomists' scorecard would be dramatic, though. If they succeeded, it would look a lot like this:

Marked For Abolition

- ✓ Estate Tax
- ✓ Interest Tax
- ✓ Dividend Tax
- ✓ Capital Gains Tax
-      Corporate Income Tax

*   *   *

The two colossal proposals—for hundreds of billions more in tax cuts, and for the new tax-free savings accounts—were introduced within weeks of each other. The Bush administration quickly narrowed its focus to the tax cuts, however. By way of explanation, Rob Nichols, the top Treasury spokesman, said that in the midst of the Congressional debate about the personal income tax cuts, everything else was secondary.

The administration's sudden shift in priorities was easy to understand. While many economists applauded the idea of removing the tax on dividends, insofar as it would remove the wedge between stocks and bonds, the overall reaction to the newly proposed tax cuts had been underwhelming.

One assessment came from Allen Sinai, chief global economist and chief executive of Decision Economics, a consulting firm. An adviser to several administrations, he was also the custodian of one of the most comprehensive models of the American economy. Perhaps more importantly, Mr. Sinai had been a guest of the White House at a big, highly publicized "economic summit" a week before the latest slate of cuts was announced.

A month later, his computers had delivered a verdict. "We've run the administration plan in its entirety through our large-scale model of the economy," Mr. Sinai said. "The impact on capital formation of the proposals being put forward by both parties looks minimal." In other words, there would be no quick arrival of the neoconomy to save the day.

It was in this atmosphere that Stephen Friedman, the new chairman of the National Economic Council and thus President Bush's top economic adviser, made his long-anticipated first public appearance. He was appointed to be a salesman, and it was time to do what Wall Street had taught him: sell, sell, sell.

Mr. Friedman finally showed his face on February 21, two months after being installed as Lawrence B. Lindsey's successor. As one might have expected at a debut, the audience seemed like it would be a friendly one. Mr. Friedman spoke in the auditorium at the Federal Reserve Bank of New York—a familiar setting for a former guru of Goldman Sachs—and to a group that consisted mainly of banking executives, economists, real estate tycoons and the odd reporter.

Though the audience initially scattered itself across about half the seats in the hall, they were soon herded down to fill up the lower rows, which happened to be in front of a television camera. Then Mr. Friedman gave a sincere if not impassioned speech about the virtues of the new plan. He appeared a little under-rehearsed, reading from a script and occasionally tripping over words that should not have given him any trouble. When the time came for questions, he was gracious, calling on members of the audience by name. No one, not even William C. Dudley, the chief United States economist at Goldman Sachs who had been a constant critic of the Bush administration's policies, asked a stumper.

But despite the careful choreographing of Mr. Friedman's debut, the audience seemed skeptical. Several people shook their heads and nudged each other as he argued that the neoconomists' latest bets would bring the fortunes of the rich and poor closer together, rather than pushing them further apart.

So much for the debut. The next time Mr. Friedman offered his views in public was two months later, to an audience of business leaders in Medford, Oregon (population: about 68,000). After that, he disappeared for months. Perhaps he had learned a lesson from his predecessor, Mr. Lindsey, who had popped up in television news shows and newspaper articles with all the regularity and jovial humor of a Teletubby. The press reported that Mr. Friedman frequently met with members of Congress to convince them of the merits of the White House's plans and to develop strategy for making them a reality. But if he was indeed the salesman for the neoconomists' bets, he certainly wasn't selling to the American voter.

*   *   *

Whatever Mr. Friedman's involvement, the neoconomists did succeed in pushing a substantial portion of their second big tax cut through Congress. In a way, they were helped by the paralysis of the economy leading up to the war in Iraq. Despite the fact that the war was also their doing, the continued job losses that preceded it helped to coax wary politicians into action.

The corporate sector had taken on such a mood of embattled weariness, in fact, that doing nothing might have seemed like a dangerous strategy for more than just political reasons. On March 15, 2003, a few days before the war with Iraq began, Norbert J. Ore, the head of the survey of factories at the Institute for Supply Management, a research group that tracks activity in the private sector, put the situation this way:

> In various industries, they're struggling to forecast the indefinite nature of the world situation. Are we going to war or are we not going to war? What's happening to energy prices and transportation costs? . . . People got to a decision point: "Do I expand and make sure I'm ready, or do I hold back?" Last year, the answer was, "I'm going to go ahead and expand and be ready." A lot of people got burned with that. This year the answer's going to be just the opposite.

Once the initial month-long push into Baghdad was over, however, optimism about the economy returned. Democrats and moderate Republicans in the Senate showed little appetite for a barrage of tax cuts as gigantic as the White House wanted; worries about the federal government's worsening finances again found voice. By the time a deal was reached with the more enthusiastic House of Representatives, the tax cuts had been reduced to a total of $320 billion.

At a cost of $162 billion, the neoconomists got most of the changes they wanted in the personal income tax: cuts in rates would be accelerated, the bias against married people filing jointly would be partly removed, and the tax credit for each dependent child would be raised to $1,000 from $600. Not all of these provisions would last, however; some were slated to expire (in election years, of course) as a way of keeping the new law's costs down.

At an additional cost of $148 billion, the neoconomists had achieved another part of their overarching strategy, just not the one they had originally sought. Rather than eliminating the tax on dividends completely, Congress settled for a compromise suggested by Republicans in the House: lowering, but not to zero, the rates on dividends *and* capital gains. From top rates of 38.6 percent (soon to be 35 percent) for dividends and 20 percent for capital gains—these applied to taxpayers with the highest incomes—the rates would fall to 15 percent. For taxpayers in the two lowest brackets, the rates would fall to just 5 percent.

The taxpayers in those two lowest brackets, with incomes of at most $28,400 per person in 2003, hardly owned any stock or other securities, anyway. But this provision allowed Congress and the White House to suggest that the new law had a progressive dimension. They focused on what percentage of people would benefit, rather than by how much. The expansion of the child tax credit allowed the administration to say it was helping working families, too. Yet there was no doubt about who the big winners would be: the people who owned the most stock, had the most capital gains, and had the highest earnings—i.e., those who would benefit from the rate cuts in every bracket, all the way up to the top.

The remaining $10 billion in the package went to businesses in the form of tax write-offs for certain purchases and properties. And yes, the changes in the new law were slated to run through 2013, into the halcyon years when surpluses were expected to return. So now, the scorecard looked like this:

Marked For Abolition

✓ Estate Tax
  Interest Tax
✓ Dividend Tax
✓ Capital Gains Tax
  Corporate Income Tax

It wasn't as impressive as the neoconomists might have hoped for, but it represented a sure step towards their ultimate destination.

*   *   *

Just days after the new tax cuts became law in May 2003, it was clear that the revolutionaries in Washington were gearing up for their next offensive. On June 2, assistant treasury secretary Pamela Olson spoke at a retirement savings conference sponsored by the Investment Companies Institute and the Securities Industry Association. The first half of her remarks was a sort of victory speech, but the second half was all about the new savings accounts—including material recycled from a speech she gave in March. "We need to go back to the drawing board," she said again. Soon, John W. Snow, her boss, was also touting the accounts once more. And in early 2004, the president would include them in the last budget proposal of his term.

The accounts were not the only prize for which the administration was preparing to fight, however. At a speech Mr. Snow gave in November 2003, he signaled the neoconomists' intent to push forward with yet more legislation. "Nothing will kill our prosperity faster than a repeal of the President's tax relief," he said, "which is scheduled to happen at the end of this decade if we don't take action now."

It was hard to believe that the Bush administration had decided only in 2003 that making the tax cuts permanent would be desirable. First the president and his allies had pushed through a ten-year package full of phase-ins and phase-outs. Then they had sped up the phase-ins. In late 2003, they declared their intention to cancel the phase-outs completely. The original $1.35 trillion plan was just a beachhead, a foothold to prepare for a bigger onslaught. In the end, the nation would be paying much more to bring about the neoconomy.

Yet again, the administration was making a grab at the future. And what revolutionary wouldn't? You don't change the tax system and the economy from top to bottom, just to let someone else reverse everything. For George W. Bush, the big decisions were too important to be left to future presidents. It wouldn't matter if they won their elections by a landslide. This president, who had won his election while losing the popular vote, was going to set the course for them.

All of this happened in less than a year. First the neoconomists had used surpluses in 2012 and 2013 to help justify their second slate of tax cuts. Then they had proposed tax-free savings accounts that would probably wipe those surpluses away. Now, they wanted to make sure that their legacy was that of all great revolutions: a permanent regime change.

Accomplishing this feat would probably require re-election for President Bush. It would also exhaust the surpluses built up in the Social Security program and require hundreds of billions, if not trillions, in extra borrowing. From the neoconomists' point of view, however, these developments would not hurt the cause. Instead, they would help the neoconomists to fight what would be the last and biggest battle in the revolution, one that they had been preparing for years to fight: the battle to privatize Social Security.

10

THE REVOLUTION IN YOUR MAILBOX

. . . rhetoric never won a revolution yet.
—SHIRLEY CHISHOLM

This chapter is about Social Security. Are you yawning yet? Thinking about skipping to the next chapter? It's true, as a topic for discussion Social Security hardly makes the pulse race. The program is an enormous bureaucracy built on a collection of numbers and arcane rules. Nevertheless, what happens to it affects all working Americans, through the taxes they pay and the retirement benefits they may someday receive. For the average middle-income worker who retires at age 65, Social Security benefits are worth hundreds of thousands of dollars, accounting for about 15 percent of all lifetime income. And as luck would have it, the fight to transform boring old Social Security was to be one of the main battles in the neoconomists' revolution.

Social Security had been one of the most contentious issues in the 2000 presidential campaign. George W.

Bush and Al Gore sparred, on the campaign trail and face to face, about how the program ought to be changed. The reason was simple: it was in trouble. But the fix that George W. Bush was offering was heavily influenced by the neoconomists and their vision.

The Social Security program had spent most of its sixty-some years as a pay-as-you-go scheme. A payroll tax would raise money from wage earners every year, and the program would then distribute that money to retired people to prevent them from slipping into poverty. Benefits rose with the cost of living. If the payroll tax rate was not high enough to pay all the benefits promised to retirees, Congress raised it. From its maturity in the late 1950's through the early 1980's, the program ran small deficits and surpluses from year to year but pretty much broke even.

In 1981, Congress and President Reagan appointed a special committee to figure out how Social Security should deal with the retirement, still two decades away, of the baby boom generation. The baby boomers were much more numerous than the generations that had come before. As a result, they could easily finance the retirement benefits for their parents' generation. But financing the baby boomers' own retirement would be a different story. It would require a big increase in the payroll taxes, a deep cut in benefits, or some other corrective measures.

The committee, headed by Alan Greenspan, recommended speeding up tax increases and pulling back some benefits in order to build up a buffer of money in the Social Security program—in essence, a fund for a day that was guaranteed to be rainy. When the baby boomers finally retired, the buffer would help to pay their benefits and hopefully remove the need for drastic action. A law passed in 1983 made the plan official, and Social Security started taking in much more than it doled out. Americans were being "overcharged" while they worked, but they were essentially paying for their own incomes in retirement.

So what was happening to all the excess money? It didn't sit idly in a vault at the offices of the Social Security Administration. The program was required to lend its surpluses to the Treasury in exchange for special IOUs. If the rest of the government ran a deficit, the Treasury could use Social Security's surpluses to make up the shortfall. Anything left over—including any regular tax revenue not spent by the Treasury—could be used to pay off the nation's debts.

Those debts included the IOUs held by Social Security, but most of them were the bonds, bills and notes the Treasury sells to the public in exchange for ready cash. Every time one of these securities came due, the Treasury had to repay the owner, in one of two ways: with tax revenue, or by selling a new security—that is, rolling over the debt like a person using one credit card to pay off another.

In January 2001, the Social Security program held about $1 trillion in IOUs from the Treasury. During the coming decade, the Congressional Budget office estimated that the program would pile up $2.5 trillion more, by handing over its extra payroll tax collections to the Treasury. In other words, the extra Social Security tax collections accounted for almost half of the $5.6 trillion in surpluses initially forecast by the budget office. The existence of these surpluses wasn't evidence that the American people had been fleeced as George W. Bush had alleged. The money had been collected deliberately, for the retirement of the baby boomers in 2010 and beyond.

The problem was, the extra surpluses wouldn't be enough to solve the problem by themselves. By 2018, the Social Security program would still be running a deficit. The White House seized on this situation to suggest transforming the entire program, a move that, incidentally, would put all those surpluses up for grabs.

To the neoconomists, it seemed, Social Security was a moneymaking machine whose sole purpose was to fund their vision. Moreover, once the program had filled the neoconomists' war chest, they planned to scrap it in favor of something completely different: a saving program that would pump hundreds of billions of dollars a year into the corporate sector, inextricably linking one of the biggest institutions in government to the neoconomy, forever.

This was probably not what Mr. Greenspan had intended. It was not what Social Security's founders had intended, either.

When Franklin D. Roosevelt signed the Social Security program into law in 1935, its main purpose was clear: to fight poverty. As the nation tried to pull itself out of economic depression, the federal government was knitting together a safety net to protect Americans of all ages from misfortune and ruin. One of the groups most at risk of falling into poverty was the elderly.

In the early 1930's, a 25-year-old American man could expect to live until he was 67.* A long, healthy retirement was far from a sure thing. Social Security probably looked something like an insurance program; just in case you lasted beyond 65, here was something that would help you out.

Indeed, being elderly and infirm was more of a risk than it ever had been before. A pamphlet circulated by the Social Security Board in 1937 hinted that the elderly had become less of an asset and more of a burden to their families:

> Old people, like children, have lost much of their economic value to a household. Most American families no longer live in houses where one can build on a room or a wing to shelter aging parents and aunts and uncles and cousins. They no longer have gardens, sewing rooms, and big kitchens where old people can help make the family's living. Old people were not "dependent" upon their relatives when there was need in a household for work they could do. They have become dependent since their room and their board

---

* Not many women were in the workforce outside the home back then, so I'm focusing on men for a moment.

cost money, while they have little to give in return. Now they need money of their own to keep the dignity and independence they had when their share in work was the equivalent in money.

In the 1930's, many people did not live long enough and could not save enough, during their working lives, to spend a decade or two in leisure. If you could retire from work, chances are you had either been extremely lucky or extremely unlucky. The lucky retirees had built wealth, perhaps by outstanding success in business or by living and working longer than the average American. The unlucky ones had been forced to stop working by infirmity. If they didn't work, it was because they couldn't work.

Obviously, no one was shedding any tears for the first group of retirees. But for the second group, who were forced into retirement, it could be a calamity. Private pensions were far from widespread, and they had none of the government-provided guarantees that they have today. Some of the retirees of the 1930's might have been able to save enough to support themselves without working, but they were exceptions rather than the rule. For the rest, the Social Security program would soften the blow by supplying them with a modest income to live on. To pay for this income, a small tax— like an insurance premium—would be taken from the wages of people who worked. The 1937 booklet explained it thus:

In general, the Social Security Act helps to assure some income to people who cannot earn and to steady the income of millions of wage earners during their working years and their old age. In one way and another taxation is spread over large groups of people to carry the cost of giving some security to those who are unfortunate or incapacitated at any one time.

The tax started out at 2 percent in 1937, not by any means a heavy burden for most working Americans. But as life expectancies lengthened and, more importantly, as successive generations became more numerous than their forebears, Social Security had to raise more money from workers to pay benefits to retirees. The ratio of workers paying into the system to people receiving benefits declined, year by year, from 16-to-1 in 1950 to about 3-to-1 in 2003. So the tax rate rose, to its current level of 12.4 percent, shared equally between companies and workers.*

By taking such a big bite out of paychecks, Social Security sucked in billions of dollars that Americans might otherwise have spent or saved. In fact, as Americans began to live longer and Social Security benefits were improved, the system became a substitute for sav-

---

* Any economist will be happy to tell you that it doesn't actually matter how much of the total tax is paid by the employer or the employee. Even if one or the other pays the entire tax, what employers pay and what employees take home will end up the same; the market will adjust the wage, whatever the situation.

ing. By 1980, the average life expectancy for a 25-year-old man was a total of 72 years. He could be fairly sure he'd make it to 65 and collect on all those contributions, so perhaps he didn't have to save so much after all.

Because paying Social Security's payroll tax was required by law, the program forcibly committed Americans to the system. Of course, it wasn't really saving, not exactly. The taxes one generation of workers paid didn't sit in an account until they retired; the taxes were collected and then paid out immediately to the retirees who were already receiving benefits. But it was still a system in which contributions in the present were rewarded with income in the future. And, loosely speaking, the more you put in—by working more years and at higher incomes—the more you'd get out.

Academic studies have offered proof that Social Security contributions mimic, and indeed replace, saving. They suggest that an extra dollar paid into Social Security can, for people whose incomes fall in some ranges, lead to a decline in saving of a dollar or more. Of course, regular saving through bank accounts and investment portfolios doesn't have the force of the law behind it; no one will go to jail for failing to put money into a mutual fund.

Still, if the studies are right, millions of Americans today are getting a raw deal. Viewed as an investment, Social Security contributions can pay an extremely crummy rate of return. To do well, you either have to live a long time and collect lots of those monthly checks, or you have to have worked for a low income during your productive years. As long as you worked for 10 years earning at least $3,600 each year, you'll still receive the fixed minimum benefit.

If you didn't fit into either of those groups, you may wish that your contributions had found their way into stocks and bonds instead of the Treasury's special accounts; the markets might have offered you a better return. And there was worse. If your spouse earned much more than you did or if you kept working through your sixties, after you became eligible for Social Security benefits, then your return on all the contributions you made could be exactly zero.

From this description, it sounds like plenty of people could simply do without Social Security. What if we turned it into a real, catastrophic insurance program again? That is, we could pay benefits only to the people who had the lowest incomes during their working lives. If we weren't going to pay benefits to all the middle class and rich folks anymore, we could cut the payroll taxes way down—all the way down to a reasonable insurance premium that could be the same for everyone. And if the studies were right, most people would take the money they would have paid into Social Security and save it themselves, laying nice little nest eggs to hatch in retirement! We could even set up accounts for everyone to help them save!

Sounds great, right? The neoconomists certainly thought so. By replacing part of the Social Security system, they could create a huge swath of new saving by households. Trillions of dollars would become available to the private sector to finance capital. And it would arrive through, of all things, a payroll tax! It would be as though the government had set up 401(k) retirement accounts for everyone, but contributing was mandatory.

This is what was meant by the oft-repeated phrase, "privatizing Social Security." What had begun as a social insurance program would end up looking more like a big mutual fund manager, feeding billions upon billions into the corporate sector. In the neoconomists' revolution, privatizing Social Security would be as big as bringing Louis XVI to the guillotine.

George W. Bush touted the benefits of privatizing part of Social Security throughout his campaign in 2000. He felt so strongly about the issue that he convened a special commission to study the program's options in May 2001. It sounded exciting—the co-chairmen were former Senator Daniel Patrick Moynihan and Richard D. Parsons, then chief operating officer of AOL/Time Warner—but it was nothing new. President Clinton and Congress had already created an advisory board to study exactly the same question in 1994. And guess what? That board had replaced an advisory council, previously convened every four years.

The advisory board, at any rate, was still in business when President Bush took office. Back in July 1998, it had offered alternatives for dealing with Social Security's impending problems in a report entitled, "Social Security: Why Action Should Be Taken Soon." At that time, the board was made up of these five people:

Stanford G. Ross (chair)—a senior partner at Arnold & Porter (a huge law firm), former president of the National Academy of Social Insurance and former commissioner of Social Security

Jo Anne Barnhart—a former Social Security Administration and Department of Health and Human Services official

Lori L. Hansen—a former Senate aide and technical assistant to the commissioner of Social Security

Martha Keys—a former congresswoman who had served on the original Greenspan commission

Sylvester J. Schieber—the director of the research and information center at Watson Wyatt (a big consulting firm specializing in human resources) and a former economic analyst at the Social Security Administration

These were no lightweights. In fact, President Bush actually nominated Ms. Barnhart to become Social Security's commissioner, which she did in November 2001. But he wasn't satisfied with their report.

It listed 14 separate types of reforms that would help to save Social Security from insolvency, but only two—creating private, individual accounts either with tax dollars or withholding from wages—conformed to the White House's main interests. The rest were pragmatic options that would not score many political points: various flavors of cutting benefits, increasing the ages of eligibility for benefits and raising taxes.

Just after President Bush took office, the board presented him with a new 55-page report entitled "Agenda for Social Security: Challenges for the New Congress and the New Administration." In it, the board again urged quick action and outlined alternative strategies. It promised to update its 1998 report with more recommendations for ensuring Social Security's long-term solvency. This, too, was all but ignored.

President Bush, it seemed, was going to have a new report that said what he wanted. Just to make sure, he changed the rules of the game. The new commission was not allowed to come to its own conclusions using its own criteria; any recommendations had to heed the president's six "Principles for Strengthening Social Security." One of these specifically prohibited putting the government's own money into the stock market. Another forbade increasing the payroll tax. That still left 12 of the advisory board's 14 options on the table. But a third "principle" read as follows: "Modernization must include individually controlled, voluntary personal retirement accounts, which will augment the Social Security safety net."

The 15 members of President Bush's commission took just three months to return an interim report with a very specific verdict: set up individual accounts.

A variety of proposals for this type of system were already circulating in the 1990's, as the magnitude of the crisis facing Social Security became increasingly clear. In some versions, individuals would decide how to invest the savings in their accounts. These proposals typically included some rules about what kinds of investments were suitable. In others, the government would choose a portfolio for everyone. Each of these options had problems, however.

In both cases, someone would have to decide which types of stocks, bonds and perhaps other kinds of securities would be allowed into the portfolio or portfolios. This was a matter of no small importance to companies and governments trying to raise money in the financial markets. Suddenly pumping trillions of dollars into a given market or sector might quickly lower the cost of capital there. If bonds of American automakers were okay but Japanese automakers' bonds were out of bounds, General Motors would gain a valuable edge over Toyota in financing new projects. If established "blue chip" stocks were fine, but new high-tech companies' shares were not, then it might become harder for innovators to enter all sorts of markets for goods and services.

Much would be at stake in those decisions. So who would make them? Almost anyone involved with the private sector would have a conflict of interest, perhaps leading them to make choices that would harm Americans' retirement plans. It was also hard to believe that a single portfolio, or a single set of rules, would be best for all Americans. For example, financial planners usually recommend riskier portfolios for younger people, to give them a shot at higher returns while they're still working. Would that sort of differentiation be possible in these plans?

Some observers expressed a deeper worry. The proposals essentially separated the saving and insurance aspects of Social Security. The program would turn into a saving vehicle, but anyone who was unable to save enough while they worked would be eligible for a minimum retirement benefit from the government. Yet if only the poor or disabled were receiving the minimum benefit, how big would that benefit be? From a political point of view, they might not be powerful enough to keep that benefit at a livable level, especially if all the payroll taxes collected by the program were no longer placed in a communal pot.

The plans' advocates often answered that these points were immaterial. Even a conservative portfolio of 60 percent American stocks and 40 percent American bonds had yielded an average return of about 5.5 percent a year, adjusted for inflation and management fees, in the past several decades. Moving money out of Social Security's special IOUs, with their interest rates that barely kept up with inflation, and into the financial markets would generate a quantum leap in the nation's retirement wealth. The details were of secondary importance.

Academic economists had conducted numerous studies, simulating possible returns in the stock market, to show that Americans' retirement savings would be safe in individual accounts. At the fore was Professor Feldstein, who had made the transformation of Social Security something of a personal crusade during the late 1990's. In a paper he authored in 1999 with Andrew

Samwick of Dartmouth College and Elena Ranguelova of Harvard, he studied how individual accounts might replace the current Social Security system.

The authors' analysis assumed that returns in the stock and bond markets would stay close to their average levels of 1946 to 1995. They concluded that individual accounts would almost always be a good deal, even for the youngest workers of the current day, who would receive no benefits under the old system. In the safest scenario the authors examined, these workers, who were 20 years old when the paper was written, would contribute 9.25 percent of their wages to individual accounts. According to the authors' simulations, there was a 50 percent chance that the workers would receive almost three times the benefits of current retirees, even adjusted for inflation, at age 70. There was a 90 percent chance that their benefits would equal at least 93 percent of the benefits being paid under the current system. And the 9.25 percent contribution they had to make was still much less than the current payroll tax of 12.4 percent. Essentially, it would take a perfect storm to ruin the plan.

Then the stock market crashed.

The Standard and Poor's 500, an index of big companies' share prices that covers about 80 percent of the market, lost exactly half its value between its high of March 2000 and its low of October 2002. In the midst of such a huge dip in the markets, and then close on its heels, it was hard to tell whether the perfect storm had indeed arrived. If stock prices had resumed their stunning rise of the 1990's, or even a slower but steady upsurge resembling the average of the past several decades, the big losses of the young millennium would soon have been erased.

But even as the nation began halting attempts at economic recovery, stocks continued to languish. The corporate scandals that had dented the public's confidence in big business did not help matters. Would the markets' sideways stumbles continue, or would they come to their senses? Under a system of individual accounts, Americans nearing their retirement would have a huge interest in the answer to that question.

Say you're 60 years old and you've worked all your life selling telecommunications equipment, the last 15 years as a manager. You won't be relying on Social Security for all your income in retirement, but it will mean the difference between living well and making sacrifices—a smaller car, a smaller house and less time spent on the beach or visiting grandchildren. Now imagine that the size of your Social Security benefit will depend on the value of a financial portfolio on the day you turn 65. You've been making contributions to that portfolio for almost 40 years, as required by the government. You haven't had much choice about the portfolio's composition, but you know what sorts of stocks and bonds are in it; the Social Security Administration sends you a report every year.

What if the stock market hit a rocky patch? You'd be checking the newspapers every day, trying to figure out what the ups and downs of the market would mean for your retirement. Without any control over buying and selling the assets in your portfolio, you'd probably feel pretty powerless, like a baseball fan futilely willing an erratic team to win. It was bad enough that the market could dip low enough to erase your benefits. But even if the portfolio did yield a slightly higher benefit than the old system would have given you, would it have been worth all the worry and stress?

There was no doubt about the effect of the market's languor on the president's hopes for transforming Social Security. The air went out of the sails. After all, what would have happened if Social Security had invested in Enron?

In a speech in March 2002, President Bush reiterated his support for individual accounts. But newspapers reported that he would delay action until after that year's Congressional elections, in hopes that the furor over corporate wrongdoing would die down.

Apparently, it didn't die down enough. The issue disappeared from the radar screen for a year. In October 2003, Joshua Bolten, the director of the White House's Office of Management and Budget, summed up the situation in the *Christian Science Monitor*: "The environment has not so far been ideal to bring forward actual legislative activity on Social Security reform."

Just a month later, however, anonymous officials

from the Bush administration deluged the media with leaks hinting that Social Security would become a big issue in the 2004 presidential campaign. Then the program disappeared from the news until President Bush mentioned it in his State of the Union address on January 20, 2004. "Younger workers should have the opportunity to build a nest egg by saving part of their Social Security taxes in a personal retirement account," he said. "We should make the Social Security system a source of ownership for the American people."

Once again, the president had put down his marker. Like tired soap operas on network television, the neoconomists' proposals never died, they just went on hiatus. The president's plan to privatize Social Security had returned, just as the plan to expand tax-free savings accounts had. But this time, there was a complication.

Alan Greenspan seized his chance to get back at the White House for squandering the surpluses his commission had created. At his testimony before the House of Representatives on February 25, 2004, Mr. Greenspan made it clear that he was not singing the same tune as the neoconomists. He pointedly outlined the problems facing Social Security, then recommended that Congress consider reducing benefits and pushing back the eligibility age. He made no mention whatsoever of individual accounts.

In the battle to transform Social Security, the neoconomists wouldn't necessarily have Mr. Greenspan on their side. They held a trump card in this game, however. Mr. Greenspan's term as chairman of the Federal Reserve ended in June 2004, and his term on the board would end in 2006. The leading candidates to replace him, should either he or the White House decide against an extension, were two highly respected academic economists: Martin S. Feldstein and R. Glenn Hubbard.

PART 3

11

CASUALTIES OF THE REVOLUTION

America's present need is not heroics but healing;
not nostrums but normalcy; not revolution but
restoration.

—WARREN G. HARDING

Almost all revolutions, even the peaceful ones, have had
their casualties. Usually, they have been outdated ideologies, the people who espoused them, and anyone
else who happened to get in the way of the new regime.

In the neoconomists' revolution, the casualties were
missed opportunities. The cost of pursuing the neoconomy was exactly equal to the benefits of the best path
not taken.

At the behest of President Bush and the neoconomists, the government committed almost all its available
resources to improving the nation's stock of capital. But
what about labor? For starters, there was little they
could do to increase the *quantity* of labor. A study
released in August 2002 by the Aspen Institute reported
that the trend most responsible for the workforce's

growth in the 1980's and 1990's—women leaving the home—had started to peter out.

In the coming decades, in fact, the fraction of the population that worked looked like it might actually fall. The Census Bureau predicted that in 2004, 65 percent of the population would be aged 16 to 64 years—the prime years for working. In 2025, the bureau projected, just 60 percent would fall into this band, as the average age of the entire population rose from 37 to 40. If a smaller share of Americans went to work, they would have to achieve markedly higher incomes in order to guarantee the living standards of the entire population.

On the other hand, there was plenty of room to improve the *quality* of labor through better education and training. The Bush administration did try to bolster the nation's schools, an effort culminating in the No Child Left Behind Act of 2001 (which actually became law in 2002). The law created a new bureaucracy for monitoring schools' performance and identifying weaknesses, and paid special attention to helping failing and disadvantaged children. Best of all, the law came with real money: about $20 to $30 billion a year.

Yet the neoconomists could have made much more dramatic changes to education had they decided to forgo some of their tax cuts. As of 2001, the nation was spending about $340 billion a year to educate children in public schools. Of that total, about $280 billion went to wages, salaries and benefits for school employees. The neoconomists' tax cuts and related initiatives cost about $154 billion a year, without taking interest payments into account. For that money, they could have increased the teaching staff by half at every public school in the nation, assuming enough qualified teachers could be found. Student-to-teacher ratios would have fallen by a third, from roughly 15-to-1 to just 10-to-1.

Alternatively, the White House could have harnessed the powerful returns of higher education. The Treasury could have begun by funding an extra year of college for any young person who wanted one. Then, once the surplus ran out, that whole generation could use some of their income gains—all thanks to the Treasury—to pay for the next generation's extra year in school. It's usually difficult to set up these subsidies between generations, since the first generation of taxpayers usually has to pay without receiving anything in return. But the anticipated budget surpluses could have solved all that.

How much would this have cost? For around $50 billion a year—less than a third of the cost of the tax cuts—the federal government could have paid enough to double first-year enrollment at the nation's four-year colleges. Failing such an ambitious plan, however, the federal government could have extended grace periods for student loans or increased tax credits for higher education, all at a substantially lower cost.

As for on-the-job training programs, the neoconomists had hardly proposed anything to match their decade-long program of tax cuts or their education initiative. In this case, the missed opportunity may have had more to do with a lack of political effort than a lack

of money. Hundreds of thousands of new workers join
the labor force each year,* but coordinating businesses
so that they valued training correctly would have cost
the government very little.

So much for improving the quality of labor—what
about innovation? President Bush did seek more money
for basic research, health and space technology in his
first three budgets.† The total budget for non-military
research in all agencies, as compiled by the National Science Foundation, rose from $41 billion in fiscal year
2001 (President Clinton's last budget) to $51 billion in
fiscal year 2004. In his fourth budget proposal, President
Bush restrained growth in research money to roughly
the rate of inflation. But the changes in the first three
years certainly loomed large in percentage terms; the
total increase amounted to about 20 percent after
adjusting for inflation.

It was nothing compared to what he could have done
with the money he committed to tax cuts.

Had he used the $154 billion a year here, he could
have *tripled* the nation's research budget. A huge,
instantaneous increase in funding for science might not

* Some of these people get help from the HOPE Scholarship and Lifetime Learning Credit, federal tax credits that can be worth several
thousand dollars a year, but neither can be used to help fund on-the-
job training or other training outside an educational institution.

† The last of the three, his fiscal year 2004 budget, did trim funding
for research on agriculture, transportation, natural resources and the
environment; funding grew in other areas.

have been the best idea, though, since it's hard to say whether the government really leaves two worthwhile projects on the drawing board for every one it funds. There simply might not be that many good projects out there. Supply and demand would play a role here, however. Chances are that after a few years of sharply rising budgets, the nation's universities would start pumping out more skilled scientists looking to follow through on their own bright ideas.

Passing up either of these types of investment—in innovation or the quality of labor—implied another cost, as well. Both of them would have committed the expected budget surpluses to government spending rather than tax cuts. And where tax cuts would be partially spent and partially saved by the people who received them, investing in the quality of labor or in innovation meant spending 100 percent of the money. All of the options came with a particular rate of return in the future, but spending—rather than cutting taxes— would have provided more of a stimulus to the economy in the short term. And that stimulus would have reduced the pain that millions of Americans felt in the early years of the new millennium.

Years had passed while the neoconomists stealthily but assiduously pursued their dream. Here was how things stood at the start of George W. Bush's re-election campaign, relative to how they were when he took office:

	January 2001	March 2004	% change
Employed people	137.8 million	138.3 million	< + 1 %
Unemployed people	6.0 million	8.4 million	+ 39 %
Unemployed people (more than 26 weeks)	0.7 million	2.0 million	+ 195 %
Current year federal surplus/deficit	$281 billion	-$478 billion	- 270 %
Projected surplus/deficit, 2002–2011	$5.6 trillion	-$2.9 trillion	- 152 %
Trade deficit (December, % of economy)	4.0 %	4.5 %	+ 14 %
Value of the dollar, in euros	1.08	0.83	- 23 %
Industrial capacity left unused (Feb. 04)	19.9 %	23.4 %	+ 18 %
Standard & Poor's 500 stock average	1373.73	1148.16	- 16 %

These were startling figures, given that, by many expert accounts, the recession of 2001 had been a relatively mild one. Even in early 2004, two million people had been looking for a job without success for more than half a year. Job creation following a recession was usually biggest in the goods-producing industrial sector. Yet the nation's industrial companies still weren't using almost a quarter of their capacity; it didn't look like they'd be starting to hire anytime soon.

Stocks were down, so people felt less wealthy. At the same time, imported goods and travel abroad were about a quarter more expensive than they had been in January 2001, because the dollar had been hammered by the euro, pound and even the yen, as Japan emerged from a decade of economic stagnation. Consumers either had to cut back on their purchases of foreign-made clothes, electronics, toys and foods, or seek out American-made alternatives that cost more to produce.

The fall in the dollar's value did convey some potentially happy news for American companies, at least for those who could export their goods and services. But the truth behind the numbers was undeniable: people had been suffering.

The first two years of the Bush administration saw a dramatic increase in the number of impoverished Americans. In 2000, there were 31.6 million people living below the federal poverty line. In 2002, there were 34.6 million. Half of that increase came among the poorest poor—those living on incomes less than half of the poverty line, or about $6.20 per person, per day for a family of four. Hunger—a condition foreign to most Americans—was also on the rise. The number of families that could not afford to buy enough food during the year, so that someone had to skip a meal, grew from fewer than 3.4 million in 2000 to 3.8 million in 2002.

The sluggish economy deserved most of the blame for these changes, which began to reverse a decade of progress in poverty reduction. But the Bush administration's policies did not attack poverty directly. Its tax cuts only offered direct aid to people who paid taxes, and that group represented only about half of the population. For people who couldn't work, or whose incomes were too low to pay taxes, the cuts offered nothing. The tax cuts would only help these people indirectly, and only to the extent that the cuts generated new jobs or more efficient ways of producing essential goods and services.

If those essential goods and services were being produced more efficiently, it wasn't necessarily showing up in lower prices. Compare these statistics from the dawn of the Bush presidency and right after the neoconomists' second big tax cut became law:

	Jan. 2001	Jun. 2003	Change
Medical care prices (index)	267.1	296.1	+ 11 %
Cost of shelter (index)	196.8	212.7	+ 8 %
Food prices (index)	170.4	179.7	+ 5 %
Gasoline price, regular	$1.38/gal	$1.43/gal	+ 4 %

Wages were rising at the same time as these prices, but that didn't do much to help the jobless or those unable to work. The Federal Reserve had cushioned the blow a bit for the average American by making credit cheaper. The low mortgage rates that resulted also kept house prices and rents high, though, so the jobless were still in for an especially rough ride.

By choosing to make tax cuts, rather than spending, the centerpiece of its economic policy during the downturn, the Bush administration offered less immediate or direct aid to the poor and jobless. This, in turn, placed a heavier burden on the states to provide a safety net. That safety net was getting a bit frayed, however, thanks to some idiosyncratic federal help.

For the people still willing and able to look for a new job, state governments provided unemployment benefits. Typically, workers could receive about half their usual weekly earnings (subject to minimums and maximums) for up to 26 weeks a year. In other words, the government would replace up to one quarter of a person's annual income. It wasn't a huge amount. In many other relatively wealthy countries, the payouts were bigger and lasted longer—in European countries, often for an unlimited time.

The cut-off in the United States has sometimes been justified by research showing that a lot of people who receive the benefits don't get new jobs until the last week or two before the benefits run out. The threat of benefits ending seems to encourage some people to find new jobs. Nevertheless, in slow economic times, the federal government has often given states extra money to prolong the payments beyond 26 weeks. The extra boost makes sense from the point of view of the labor market; it's not the worker's fault that finding a job has become that much more difficult.

Three years after the recession of 2001, the job market was still soft. In the meantime, Congress and the White House had extended unemployment benefits for hundreds of thousands of the jobless. But they had also hung many others out to dry.

The first extension of unemployment benefits, passed as part of the Job Creation and Worker Assistance Act of 2002, was designed to go into effect on March 10, 2002, six months after the terrorist attacks. If you had lost your job before the attacks, and your 26 weeks of benefits had already run out—after all, the recession supposedly started in March 2001—you were out of luck. You'd have to wait until March 10 to pick up any new checks.

Later in 2002, the extended unemployment benefits hit another speed bump. They were scheduled to expire on December 28, and the Senate passed a bill to extend them again. But the House didn't send the bill to the president's desk until 11 days later, leaving thousands of people without checks right after the big holiday spend.

All through 2003, legions of jobless Americans were exhausting even the extended unemployment benefits paid for by the federal government. According to estimates compiled by the National Employment Law Project and the Democratic staff of Congress's Joint Economic Committee, about 1.4 million people had used up their benefits without finding a job by October 2003. The analysts estimated that a further million would find themselves in the same situation by March 2004.

A little restraint in granting more benefits made sense, at least given the economic evidence. In addition, the spectacular growth of the economy in the third quarter of 2003—at an annual rate of 8.2 percent—suggested that jobs would soon become available for some of those who wanted them. But there was no doubt that hundreds of thousands of people had been struggling to get by for many months.

For the people who had lost their jobs, there was almost always an extra dose of bad news: chances were they lost their health insurance, too. Federal law allowed them to stay in their former employers' health insurance pools for up to 18 months, but only by paying the full premium. The jobless could not count on their former employers to pick up most of the tab. And that's where the sticker shock came in.

Typically, workers paid only 10 to 20 percent of their health insurance premiums, with employers stepping in to pay the rest. An economist might have argued that the employer took some of its share out of the workers' wages. But once workers were let go, there was no ambiguity; they had to pay 100 percent themselves, up to hundreds of dollars a month. To make matters worse, most workers couldn't switch into a less expensive plan except during one month of the year. Many who opted to extend their coverage couldn't switch at all.

Experts in Washington estimated that only about 5 percent of low-income people chose to extend their health insurance after losing their jobs. About 20 percent became eligible for Medicaid, offered through state governments, and another quarter could have received coverage through their spouses' jobs—something much more common in higher income ranges. But about half, along with their dependents in many cases, seemed likely to end up uninsured. Overall, 900,000 full-time workers lost their coverage in 2002.

Why did so many slip through the cracks? The cost of extending coverage was certainly prohibitive. Even for a single person in a health maintenance organization (HMO), where premiums are typically lower than in other types of insurance, coverage cost an average of $174 a month, or $40 a week. During the same period, the average weekly benefit paid by unemployment insurance was about $250. Was it worth paying $40 of your $250 income just for health insurance? How about $116 a week for the average family insurance plan?

That wouldn't leave too much for housing or food. And by the way, those unemployment benefits were taxable.

At the same time, the state governments that paid benefits needed to save money. All of them except Indiana and Vermont had some sort of rule requiring balanced budgets every year. Even though they had been swimming in tax revenue during the booming 90's, they hadn't stashed enough of it away to deal with the stagnant 00's. The reason was a combination of politics and good, old-fashioned American overoptimism.

First, the politics. It's always hard for a government to save up surpluses, as the Bush administration itself demonstrated, because there's always a temptation to return the money to voters in the form of tax cuts. The same maxim holds at every level, from a town council up through Washington: even if the current government wants to keep hold of its surpluses, chances are that its challengers at the next election will promise to break open the vaults on behalf of the taxpayers. And, to be fair, it's not just the taxpayers who want the money. Unions of state employees, contractors for state construction projects, local school systems—they all clamor for more cash, too.

The task of government saving was made even more difficult in the 1990's, however, by the relentless optimism of the era. Ten years into the longest boom in recorded history, some forecasters had wondered aloud whether Alan Greenspan and Robert E. Rubin had finally dealt the economic cycle a deathblow. Needless to say, those forecasters turned out to be wrong. All the same, it was not completely surprising that the recession of 2001 caught many state governments unawares.

Overoptimism might have left states in the lurch, but, in a world of fiscal balance, wouldn't the problem have been solved in next year's budget? Not exactly. Having a governor sign a balanced budget doesn't always mean that the books will add up at the end of 12 months. It didn't matter how much a state planned to spend; if the amount of revenue coming in was not what the government expected, it would still come up short. And it was not unheard of for forecasters and politicians to make this sort of mistake two years in a row.

Even in 2002, after the recession had supposedly ended, states were having trouble making ends meet. Towards the end of the year, more than 40 states found that they would have to make up for shortfalls by trimming their budgets for 2003. Just like the companies that had been burned by expectations of a recovery in the summer of 2002, the states reluctantly took it upon themselves to rein in spending, often with across-the-board cuts.

After making $13.7 billion in cuts during fiscal year 2002, the states made plans to slash another $14.5 billion in fiscal year 2003. Each year's cuts represented enough money to educate almost 2 million kids in public schools, at the average cost per pupil, or to give comprehensive health insurance to more than 2 million families. At least 24 states either cut funds for education during fiscal year 2002 or planned to do so in fiscal year 2003. At least 30 cut funds for medical care or health insurance. At least 33 even cut money for public safety. And 11 states cut every program they had. Oklahoma's constitution actually required proportional cuts in all state programs, with no exceptions.

Allotting less money for public safety was a tough choice at a time when terrorism, at least in states with big cities and business centers, still seemed like a threat. But cuts in health care, welfare (in some states) and especially education would arguably have the greatest long-term consequences. In most cases, you only had one chance to teach a child the fourth grade. What he learned would affect his productivity and his contribution to the economy for the rest of his life. So would what he ate, and whether he was treated for childhood diseases. The states found themselves being forced to cut back on all sorts of programs at a time when, at least in cases like health insurance, their citizens needed them most.

The states begged Washington for cash several times, culminating in a visit to Washington by the National Governors Association in February 2003. The governors predicted that the states would suffer budget shortfalls totaling $80 billion in 2004. But the Bush administration was fairly unsympathetic to their pleas. Helping the needy—whether people or governments—implied two trade-offs. The first was obvious: spend money on the needy today, and you'd have less to spend on other things, either today or tomorrow. The second was not as clear: spend money on the needy now, and people might not look at being needy as such a bad thing.

No phrase could have conveyed these trade-offs better than "compassionate conservatism," the motto that George W. Bush adopted during his presidential campaign. To aid the needy during the economy's dip was surely compassionate; to curtail that aid in the name of discipline was most definitely conservative.

Forcing the states to be self-sufficient—and to feel the bite of their balanced budget rules—might have encouraged their legislators to be more thrifty in the future. Perhaps, with a sufficient dose of this tough love, they would save enough during booms to make sure that busts didn't bring more trips to Washington with hats in hand. The message was clear: ride it out, learn your lesson.

But hold on a just a minute, you might be thinking: wasn't the White House using an opposite logic to justify its own programs? Didn't the neoconomists say that balanced budgets could always wait until the economy was back on its feet?

Economists—especially Keynesians—would have agreed that incurring deficits during bad times is okay, as long as they help to lessen hardship and speed up recovery; you can, and should, pay them back when times are good again. This logic couldn't be applied to the states, since it wasn't traditionally their job to provide the spark for the economy. But they did have something to say about lessening hardship through programs like unemployment insurance, Medicaid and welfare. By focusing on tax cuts, Washington had left most of the job of protecting the poor and jobless to the states—wasn't there an implied obligation to help them with the task at hand?

At the last moment of negotiations between the House and Senate, the two sides agreed to add $20 billion over two years to the Jobs and Growth Tax Relief Reconciliation Act of 2003 for the purpose of bailing out the states. It was a drop in the bucket in the context of the new law, which would cost $350 billion in total over the coming decade, but it did pick up much of the states' shortfalls.

The compromise would certainly help those in need in 2003. For the people who suffered in 2001 and 2002, the money came too late; the damage was done. In any event, the White House could argue that the conservative side of compassionate conservatism forbade it from doing more to help the needy directly.

But this was a hollow excuse, at least to the extent that the White House's policies—so focused on the long term—had worsened the pain for the economy's unfortunates. It was as though your best friend started a fire by accident in your house, then refused to put it out. You might have been curious to know why he let your house burn down. And this was his explanation: "If I hadn't, you might have figured that you never needed to buy insurance!"

In many ways, this was also the Bush administration's message to the millions of Americans who became poor and unemployed during the slump that began in early 2001. The White House could have lent them more of a helping hand in so many ways, resulting in tangible economic benefits. Calls for extended unemployment payments, targeted tax cuts and aid to the states made the headlines. More pro-active food support, subsidized health insurance and any other measures that the sharp minds in Washington would have come up with, had they ever put their minds to it, could also have created economic value. But the Bush administration had weighed up the options, and its choice was clear: whatever the benefits to society of easing the pain today, the pursuit of the neoconomy remained the top priority.

12

REALITY, OR STILL A DREAM?

The successful revolutionary is a statesman, the unsuccessful one a criminal.

—ERICH FROMM

Imagine that it's 2012.

George W. Bush served two terms as president, during which he eliminated all taxes on savings and wealth. He also passed a constitutional amendment allowing foreign-born citizens to become president. The winner of the presidential election in 2008, Arnold Schwarzenegger, made sure to maintain all his predecessor's economic policies.

What does the economy look like in 2012? If the neoconomists were right, it's a pulsating capitalist machine. Americans' incomes have risen so much that they can spend more and save *much* more at the same time. Economic growth is averaging around 4 percent a year, as opposed to the middling 3's of the previous half-century.

All the fiscal imbalances of George W. Bush's first

term have disappeared. Tax collections are growing every year alongside the booming economy, and deficits have turned into surpluses, even without taxes on savings and wealth. The government has started to defray its debts again, and long-term interest rates are falling. And with smaller debts and lower interest rates, the federal government is not spending as much on interest payments to creditors. There's more money for Medicare, national security, education and all the other things Americans care about.

Moreover, foreigners can see that the United States has once more become, unquestionably, the world's most attractive target for investment. Even China and India, darlings of the dawn of the millennium, cannot match the safe, high returns in the United States. And by making more money available to finance American companies' projects, foreigners are helping the neoconomy to gather speed.

Yet this inflow of money from abroad has not resulted in a gaping trade deficit. Giant leaps forward in technology, spurred by businesses' investment in research and development, have whetted the foreign appetite for American exports like never before.

Even though thousands of jobs in service professions have moved overseas, the nation's powerful engine of innovation—imagine fifth-generation mobile phones, microscopic housecleaning robots, computer chips made of organic molecules and artificial bones made of carbon nanotubes—has produced an insatiable demand for American labor. That "labor" isn't the kind people used to talk about in the heyday of manufacturing, with sweaty men and kerchief-wearing women working on assembly lines and construction sites. No, this labor sits in front of high-powered computers, in chemistry labs and in the boardrooms of companies all around the world.

The unemployment rate has fallen to record lows, and the stock market has risen to record highs. Riding the stock market's wave have been the millions of retirees whose Social Security contributions have been invested in the nation's companies. Forced to save by the system, they have reaped the rewards in the form of monthly checks made out in dizzyingly high amounts. Where the elderly used to be a burden on their families, now every kid seems to have a sugar grandma or sugar granddaddy.

America has not just held onto the title of the world's leading economy, it has clenched that title with a steel claw. At the same time as it has reduced its debts to the rest of the world, it has strengthened its own ability to control resources around the globe. The 1990's were nothing. This is the real era of American economic supremacy.

But not every revolution ends the way its plotters planned, no matter how cocksure they are.

Back in George W. Bush's presidency, the neoconomists and the other members of the administration exuded a confidence bordering on certainty when they described the effects of their policies. There was no better demonstration of this confidence than the following statement released in an e-mail by Rob Nichols, the chief Treasury spokesman:

> By the end of 2004, had there not been the fiscal stimulus measures proposed by President Bush: The unemployment rate would be as much as 1.6 percentage points higher. The economy would have created as many as 3 million fewer jobs. Real gross domestic product would be as much as 3.5 to 4 percent lower.

The odd thing about this statement was that Mr. Nichols issued it on July 15, 2003. Even allowing for the looseness of e-mail grammar, it was clear that Mr. Nichols was, in 2003, speaking about events in 2004 as though they were etched-in-stone certainties. Mr. Nichols's confidence was based not on any personal clairvoyant ability but on the Council of Economic Advisers' computer model of the economy. The model's predictions were always subject to a margin of error, which, incidentally, neither the council nor Mr. Nichols reported. But there was a bigger problem with Mr. Nichols' statement: the computer model did not *predict* that tax cuts would lead to new jobs; the model *assumed* it.

Because economic models are based on mathematical logic, their creators can gain a robust, and sometimes excessive, confidence in their conclusions. If A + B = C, and we increase B by a little bit, surely C will increase by a little bit, too. Just as in physics—a field in which several of the most respected economists began their studies—models give strict predictions of how the world will behave.

Yet economics is not physics. The cornerstones of modern physics are indisputable truths—they're even called laws—that fit all the known dynamics of the universe. If a law is ever shown to be incorrect, or even just an approximation as opposed to an exact relationship, it is a watershed event.

In economics, every single model is based on assumptions. Most of the assumptions are intended to simplify the world so that it may be explained by a few equations. These equations, once assembled, have the elegance of mathematics and the inexorability of its logic. They are usually tested using data from the economy, as are new conjectures in physics, to see how well they fit reality. If they don't fit, they are thrown out or recalibrated. But even if they fit the data for one economy during one period of time, there's no guarantee that they will fit in the future, in that same economy or anywhere else. As a result, making predictions in economics can be even more difficult than forecasting the weather.

Part of the reason is that the data that underlie economic models represent a quagmire of assumptions and approximations. The best balances can precisely measure the mass of an object weighing about a gram to within a millionth of a gram.* If the same were true of

---

* For example, the Sartorius MC5 balance.

the size of gross domestic product—the total value of all goods and services made in the United States—then the government's estimates would be precise to within $10,000. But when the Bureau of Economic Analysis tries to gauge gross domestic product using different techniques—for example, by comparing production of goods and services to the income generated by their sale—the results can vary by as much as $100 billion, or 1 percent of the total. And the bureau is one of the most advanced data collectors in the world.

More importantly, however, there is no innate reason why any economy should be governed by unchanging laws. Unlike the physical universe, ruled by atoms whose behavior has not wavered since they sprang out of some cosmic mush, the economy is composed solely of people and the resources they can use. As their behavior changes, so might the rules of the economy.

Even trying to answer an apparently simple question can make your head spin within seconds. For example, take the question of whether raising personal income tax rates will make people work more, or less. The answer is likely to be very different, depending on what the tax rates are now, what they will be after the change, and the people in question.

If the tax rates start low and are raised by a tiny increment, chances are that few people will change their behavior. If taxes are raised to nearly 100 percent,*

* In Communist countries, where the government supplied education, health care, shelter and entertainment, this system did work . . . for a while.

though, people might not bother showing up for work at all. What's the point, if the government takes almost everything away?

In many ways, a *moderate* increase in taxes is the hardest to judge. Consider its effects on three different people. A single mother whose one job supplies just enough money to pay the rent might actually work more after the rates rise; she has to put in more hours for the same take-home pay. The target for her income is non-negotiable—it's income or eviction.

A successful entrepreneur facing the higher rates might decide to cut back on his work time and play more golf. He already has plenty of money, thanks to the patent on his whiz-bang invention. Since the amount of extra money he can earn by working more has declined, he might prefer to indulge in more leisure.

An immigrant laborer who works three jobs to make ends meet might not change his labor pattern at all, either because he's paid under the table (and therefore outside the tax system) or because there simply aren't any more hours to work in the day. And with three jobs, you can bet he'll need his sleep.

On the other hand, all of these analyses could be wrong. Maybe the single mother will decide to move to a less expensive area of town, so she can still spend just as much time with her kids. Perhaps what drives the entrepreneur to work more is his passion for innova-tion—not money—and the tax rates will make no differ-ence. And perhaps the immigrant laborer won't be able to find work as easily, because the higher tax rates will mean the people he works for will have less money to spend.

Even if lower taxes on wages do encourage people to work more, there's a limit to the effect: the maximum number of hours you can work in a day is, despite occasional protestations to the contrary, fixed at 24.* The same was true for the neoconomists' main target—saving. If you save everything you earn, you have nothing left to spend on essentials like food and shelter, let alone fun stuff like concert tickets and trips to Tahiti.

The size of the increase in living standards that would result from the neoconomists' policies would depend on how much the saving rate rose. Yet just as higher wages don't guarantee that people will work more, a higher return on stocks and bonds would not necessarily guarantee more saving.

The saving decision is extremely complex. It depends not just on interest rates and incomes but also on people's motives—not always the easiest things to put in a mathematical model. In the past decade or so, economists have begun working with psychologists to understand these motives. Still, standard economic theory does offer a starting point for analyzing the decision to save or not, and if so, how much.

According to the theory, a person might react to an increase in the return to saving—i.e., what happens

* Here I am thinking especially of Run-DMC, whose 1985 hit "You Talk Too Much" spoke of 25 hours in a day, eight days in a week and 13 months in a year.

when saving becomes tax-free—in two ways. The first way basically amounts to the person saying, "Hey, now each dollar I save earns a bigger return! That means spending money today implies giving up *more* spending in the future than it did before! I think I'll spend less today and save more!" The second way goes like this: "Hey, now each dollar I save earns a bigger return! Now I don't have to save as much in order to go ahead with the spending I planned for the future! I think I'll save less today and spend more!"

People could react in the first way, the second way or a combination. It's hard to predict, because reasons for saving can change rapidly. In the Federal Reserve's Survey of Consumer Finances for 1992, 22 percent of people who reported saving cited retirement as the most important reason. When the Federal Reserve conducted the same survey in 2001, 34 percent of people who reported saving said they did so to prepare for retirement. So how would these people react to a higher return on saving? They might jump at the chance to guarantee themselves a higher income after they stop working, by saving more. Or they might be aiming for a set target—say an income of $30,000 a year. In that case, a higher return to saving would mean they did not have to save as much; they could spend more in the present.

The past decade has offered plenty of reason to believe in the latter, perhaps less intuitive, motivation. In the late 1990's, the stock market rocketed upwards and bonds paid fairly high returns in an environment of very little inflation. Returns to saving were extremely high, yet Americans saved only a tiny fraction of the money they earned. The values of their *existing* portfolios were growing so quickly that there seemed to be little reason to sock *more* money away; spending it in the here and now was more attractive. After all, there was no guarantee that they'd even be around tomorrow to take advantage of their saving. And not everyone wanted to leave a big bequest.

Another problem was that the United States was not, in an economic as well as a geographical sense, an island. Americans were perfectly capable of investing their savings overseas, if they saw fit. In the extreme case—for example, if everyone decided that China offered better opportunities than the United States—the nation's own capital stock wouldn't see any improvement at all from lower taxes on saving.

As discussed earlier, people in most rich countries have typically invested the bulk of their savings at home, and not everyone knows what opportunities are available abroad. Nevertheless, the preference for investing at home has been eroding slowly with the greater globalization of financial markets. Remember, once upon a time most Americans had never heard of sushi. Now some of them prefer it to hamburgers.

Another source of uncertainty shadowing the extra saving that would fuel the neoconomy had to do with the government's finances. If the government needed to borrow more and more money during the period when saving increased, then it was unlikely that all the money set aside by households would find its way into the corporate sector. Some would undoubtedly find a home in Washington.

Uncertainty surrounded the effect the pursuit of the neoconomy would have on innovation, too. Richard H. Clarida, the assistant secretary of the Treasury for economic policy from September 2001 until May 2003, was one of the neoconomists who believed in the payoff—that companies would use some of the new financing available to them for research and development, leading to faster technological change. Still, when interviewed in early 2003, he declined to predict the size of the effect: "We expect that it would be positive," he said, "but we're still in the process of quantifying what that would be."

Professor Clarida's reticence was understandable. It was a little like a weather forecaster trying to predict exactly when the next Ice Age would begin. Yes, it would happen sometime in the future, and it would probably be pretty cold, but beyond that one couldn't really say for sure.

So after three years chasing the vision of the neoconomy, what was the bottom line? The Bush administration committed about $1.7 trillion of the nation's resources to the pursuit, and the potential return on that investment had three components: (1) the removal of resources from a supposedly wasteful government, (2) economic growth from an expanding capital stock and a faster pace of innovation and (3) economic growth from people working more as a result of lower tax rates.

The size of the first component—the benefits from simply yanking dollars out of Washington—was hard to measure.* But in terms of the success of the neoconomy, this component was also the least meaningful. If the government did indeed waste money, *any* tax cuts that resulted in less government spending would have the same benefits, even if they had nothing to do with the neoconomy.

As for the second and third components of the return, the Congressional Budget Office didn't seem too convinced that either of them would ever appear. In January 2004, it had predicted faster economic growth for 2004 and 2005 on the strength of the tax cuts and the bounce-back from the economy's three-year slump. But the budget office apparently didn't buy the idea that in the long-term, the tax cuts would transform the economy into a more efficient, capital-rich, constantly innovating utopia. Its forecast for growth in 2006–2011 was just 2.7 percent, hardly enough to create new jobs. Back in January 2001, before all the tax cuts, the budget

---

* According to an ABC News/*Washington Post* poll taken in April 2002, Americans believed, on average, that the federal government wasted 47 cents of every dollar it spent ("Evaluating the IRS," ACNews.com, April 15, 2002). Americans have also been known to overestimate the size of the nation's budget for foreign aid by 20-fold, as reported by the Program on International Policy Attitudes at the University of Maryland ("Americans on Foreign Aid and World Hunger," February 2, 2001).

office's forecast for growth in those same years was 3.1 percent.

The budget office's skepticism was understandable, given the context. The neoconomists had consistently overpredicted the economic benefits of their policies. Every February, the Council of Economic Advisers forecast how the nation's payrolls would grow over the coming years. And its forecasts for 2002, 2003 and 2004 all proved to be wrong—too optimistic by millions of jobs in each case.

Part of the discrepancy came from the fact that Congress had not passed all the tax cuts that the White House had requested. For example, President Bush had to make do with a tax cut of $350 billion in 2003, though the initial version written up by the House would have cost $726 billion. But the result of the tax cut being chopped in half was not that the job growth predicted by the council was also chopped in half. Until early 2004, there was virtually no job growth at all.

The Bush administration argued that unforeseen problems in the economy had held the job market back, and that its policies still made the situation better than it otherwise would have been. There was no way to prove this claim, however, and it began to take on a tired ring. It was possible that the tax cuts simply weren't having the effects that the neoconomists predicted. Either way, it seemed pointless to base any decisions on the council's forecasts.

A stunning coincidence drove home this last point. On March 9, 2004, *The New York Times* and its rival, the

Wall Street Journal, each printed an opinion piece by an expert economist. In the *Times,* it was by Paul Krugman, a Princeton professor who had written a column in the newspaper for years. In the *Journal,* it was by Robert Barro, a Harvard professor and frequent contributor who wrote a column in *BusinessWeek.* These two men stood at opposite ends of the political spectrum. In the run-up to the presidential election in 1996, they had debated each other on the Public Broadcasting System's *NewsHour,* with Professor Krugman supporting Bill Clinton's policies and Professor Barro backing Bob Dole. They had debated George W. Bush's tax cuts in January 2003 on PBS's *Wall $treet Week,* with Professor Barro for and Professor Krugman against.

Yet on this occasion, the two professors were singing the same tune, if in slightly different keys. They both wrote that the Council of Economic Advisers' latest forecast—for a gain of more than 3 million jobs in 2004, based on that same model of the economy—was unlikely at best. "Economic forecasting isn't an exact science, but wishful thinking on this scale is unprecedented," Professor Krugman wrote. Professor Barro reported that his own mathematical model of the economy predicted a *loss* of 1.5 million jobs from February 2004 to February 2005. "Frankly, I anticipated a more favorable outlook for year-ahead employment growth," he wrote.

All was not lost, however. The neoconomists were, after all, blazing their own trail. Never before, except in economics textbooks, had a wealthy nation attempted to lower its taxes on saving so dramatically and so quickly.* The plan was unique and unprecedented, and so was the setting.

In the well-oiled machine of the American economy, people could be expected to act on their best capitalist impulses—the kind that make most economic models work. Basic incentives seemed sure to play a bigger role than they would in Europe, Japan or other countries more hampered by regulation and huge public sectors. What's more, the models the neoconomists used to predict the outcomes of their bets were almost universally constructed by Americans, or at least by foreign academics sitting at desks in America, often with an American-style economy in mind.

These, at least, were reasons for optimism. But even if the neoconomists were right all along, there was still a chance that their dream would become America's nightmare.

---

* The country that comes closest is probably Canada. It is in the midst of a five-year tax-cutting plan, which, among other things, lowers the tax rate on corporate profits by a quarter (to 21 percent from 28 percent) and exempts a substantial share of capital gains from tax. Ireland experienced still more dramatic changes in the 1990's, with tax rates falling even further. But the cuts were accompanied by vast changes in regulation of industry, competition policy, labor markets and foreign investment. Comparability is further damaged by the fact that the Irish economy is about a hundredth the size of the American economy. In addition, economic theory predicts that in a group of industrialized countries, those with lower standards of living (e.g., Canada and Ireland) will grow faster as they catch up to the one with the highest standard of living (e.g., the United States).

13

REVOLUTION BEGETS REVOLUTION

> In the nature of things, those who have not prop-
> erty, and see their neighbors possess much more
> than they think them to need, cannot be favorable
> to laws made for the protection of property. When
> this class becomes numerous, it grows clamorous.
> It looks on property as its prey and plunder, and is
> naturally ready, at all times, for violence and revo-
> lution.
>
> —DANIEL WEBSTER

If the neoconomists' revolution succeeded, the neoconomy would arrive along with the bigger economic pie
they had promised. But this radical change in the way
we live would deliver other, more troubling consequences, too. There could be some nasty side effects to
the arrival of the neoconomy. Considering what the
neoconomy would really be like, the new regime could
set processes in motion that would eventually lead to its
destruction.

First, the side effects. Though the Bush administration never admitted it, its tax cuts would almost certainly push the incomes of rich and poor further apart.
As incomes became more widely dispersed, the gap in
wealth between rich and poor would quickly grow as

well. Even to a non-economist, the reason was easy to see: all the tax cuts that had to do with the neoconomy were supposed to raise the return to saving—not just new saving, but existing saving, too—and the rich had much more saving than the poor.

In 2010, all the provisions of the 2001 tax cuts would finally be implemented. A few figures can illustrate how they would affect the distribution of income and wealth, after federal income taxes were paid. First, consider the changes in how much after-tax income different groups of taxpayers would control:

	Change in share of all after-tax income in 2010 (with phase-outs)	Change in share of all after-tax income in 2010 (without phase-outs)
Top 20 percent of taxpayers	+ 0.5 %	+ 1.0 %
Second 20 percent	- 0.2	- 0.4
Middle 20 percent	- 0.1	- 0.3
Fourth 20 percent	- 0.0	- 0.2
Bottom 20 percent	- 0.1	- 0.1

These don't look like particularly big numbers. But consider the actual amounts of money involved, and the effects begin to appear more impressive:

	Total added after-tax income in 2010 (with phase-outs)	Total added after-tax income in 2010 (without phase-outs)
Top 20 percent of taxpayers	$163 billion	$356 billion
Second 20 percent	31 billion	47 billion
Middle 20 percent	23 billion	26 billion
Fourth 20 percent	15 billion	16 billion
Bottom 20 percent	3 billion	3 billion

Perhaps the most revealing expression of the data is the one that makes the most straightforward comparison of individual taxpayer to individual taxpayer. Look at the change in the after-tax income of *each* tax filer in 2010:

	Added after-tax income in 2010 (with phase-outs)	Added after-tax income in 2010 (without phase-outs)
Top 20 percent of taxpayers	$5,725	$12,462
Second 20 percent	1,081	1,662
Middle 20 percent	791	925
Fourth 20 percent	508	562
Bottom 20 percent	98	114

Finally, see just how much those differences mean as they accumulate over the entire ten-year period:

	Change in wealth: total tax cut, 2001–2010 (with phase-outs)	Change in wealth: total tax cut, 2001–2010 (without phase-outs)
Top 20 percent of taxpayers	$46,243	$73,002
Second 20 percent	10,453	12,893
Middle 20 percent	6,516	7,387
Fourth 20 percent	4,037	4,413
Bottom 20 percent	827	947

The tax cuts might make the overall pie bigger. But they would also shift a big slice of that pie up to the highest earners.

Over time, this shift in income would be reflected by much bigger shifts in wealth. The people in the top 20 percent had incomes averaging 4.5 times the incomes of the people in the middle 20 percent, yet the tax cuts would be worth more than *seven* times as much to the high earners. And for the very highest earners—those in the top one percent—the tax cuts would mean extra wealth of more than half a million dollars each.

This effect could have been even more pronounced, had the tax cuts in 2001 and 2003 not included lower rates for wages at all levels of income. But the neoconomists' further plans included no more such cuts. After permanently abolishing the estate tax, as well as taxes on capital gains, interest payments, dividends and other corporate profits—the tax-free saving accounts by themselves would go a long way in this direction—disparities in after-tax incomes would only widen.

Philosophers, pundits and politicians have argued that increases in income inequality don't matter too much, as long as living standards for the poorest keep rising. It is true that, as long as the wages of low-income people keep up with increases in prices, those people will be able to keep buying as much food, shelter and other necessities as they did before. But their access to opportunities may differ.

That can be a problem. In a world driven solely by economic efficiency, the young people with the highest aptitudes for leading productive lives would receive the most education and training, so that society might best exploit their talents. In America, it doesn't always work that way. Children who grow up in poor areas typically have access to fewer resources—books, activities, teachers' and parents' time—during early schooling than their wealthier counterparts. Many colleges try to account for these differences when deciding which kids to admit, but not all do. Not every college's admissions policies ignore students' financial needs, either. Even some of the best private colleges, like Brown University, have been forced by budget problems to abandon their need-blind admissions policies from time to time.*

This is where the extent of inequality matters. The greater the distance between rich and poor, in terms of resources, the more likely a not-so-bright, rich kid will take a place at college from a smart, poor kid. The same goes for other sorts of opportunities where people compete for a limited number of slots. Which candidate for city council is more likely to make it through the primary—the one with a personal fortune to use in the campaign, or the one without?

As long as money mediates access to opportunities, inequality will continue to create economic inefficiencies. The talents of the smart but poor will be partially lost to the economy, misallocated in low-paying, low-skilled jobs without much scope for creativity or innovation.†

When this issue is discussed in Washington, it is usually a sense of compassion that compels politicians to

---

* For several years, Brown University admitted about 90 percent of its undergraduate classes without considering students' ability to pay, then filled the rest of the spots with those who could afford full tuition and fees. Brown instituted a fully need-blind policy for the Class of 2007.

† There are some who believe that people who are born into poor backgrounds are less likely to have the "smart" gene, if such a gene exists. I'm not scientifically qualified to discuss that claim, but my experiences teaching undergraduates at Harvard belie it. I'm going to assume that a substantial number of children born into poverty have the raw materials to become big contributors to the economy.

try, for example, to fight poverty among children. Yet there are especially pressing *economic* reasons to worry about squandering the potential of a good-sized chunk of the labor force. Such waste—which is probably going on already, but would almost certainly grow along with inequality if not addressed soon—would threaten *all* Americans' living standards in very tangible ways.

Start at the top. Big-time investors depend on returns to capital for their paychecks; they benefit when stock prices and interest rates (adjusted for inflation) rise. But in a world with a stagnant labor force, what will happen to their profits? With more and more capital piling up, the only way to keep profits growing will be to improve the intangibles: innovation in technology and management, and the education and skills of workers.* It's already clear that educated workers will command a premium; as businesses compete to hire them, more corporate profits will end up as their wages, rather than as dividends for investors. But rising inequality could threaten both innovation and education.

When inequality grows, and resources for education and training are misallocated, it is likely that gains in workers' productivity will slow. The workers with the best training won't necessarily be the brightest, and fewer bright minds will find themselves in a position to follow up on their best ideas. This turn of events will slow increases in investors' returns on capital as well,

---

* Some readers may have heard the latter items referred to collectively as "human capital."

since the economy will not be devoting its best resources to discovering new technologies and new ways to work. And since the wealthy tend to be the biggest investors, they are the ones who could suffer most of all.

Academic economists have already begun to discuss this problem. Some are forecasting an economic cataclysm in the United States, as Thomas Piketty, director of the School for Advanced Studies in the Social Sciences (EHESS) in Paris, did in April 2003:

> These new high-income tax cuts, together with all the previous tax cuts (including the repeal of the estate tax), will eventually contribute to rebuild a class of rentiers in the U.S., whereby a small group of wealthy but untalented children controls vast segments of the U.S. economy and penniless, talented children simply can't compete. . . . If such a tax policy is maintained, there is a decent probability that the U.S. will look like Old Europe prior to 1914 in a couple of generations.

The mismatch of resources to talent may not turn out to be quite so dire as Professor Piketty projected; tax cuts are not the only thing that will affect who gets to do what in the economy.* Yet rising inequality presents a further threat to the economy's realization of its innate

---

* See J. Bradford DeLong's weblog on April 20, 2003 (at www.j-bradford-delong.net) for a short rebuttal. Professor DeLong does not, however, contest a central finding of Professor Piketty's research: that the shares of income in the hands of the highest-earning Americans are bigger now than at any time since the 1920's.

NEOCONOMY

genius. Even if the nation manages to nurture talent in poor environments, inequality could render that talent's owners reluctant or unable to use it.

Academic economists have identified the ability to own the fruits of one's labors as an important incentive behind innovation. In an unequal society, however, achieving that ownership becomes more difficult. Gathering up the materials and money to start a new venture is no easy thing for people who are poor to begin with, especially when many wealthier people are also in line. It's much easier for them to sell their ideas to someone with the wherewithal to follow through—settling for a small up-front payoff in lieu of a long stream of profit. And when the rewards of creativity and innovation seem so far off as to be unreachable, what is the point of pursuing them? To the extent inequality demoralizes, it results in more wasted ability.

Inequality can have other damaging effects on the economy, too. People care not just about how much they have, but also about how much they have relative to other people in society. When the gap between the haves and the have-nots grows, it's natural that the have-nots become less satisfied and, perhaps, more restless. During the 1980's, as taxes fell and the economy boomed, the gap in incomes between the top 5 percent of families (ranked by income) and the bottom 20 percent stretched from 11-fold to 15-fold. Greed and excess became more accepted and even sometimes lauded parts of American culture. Was it a coincidence that more teenagers from poor neighborhoods joined drug gangs that held out the promise of big money, big jewelry and big cars?

Using data covering the 1970's through 2000, a team at Princeton University found evidence for a strong link between inequality and imprisonment rates in the past few decades. "Incarceration rates increased most among those whose economic losses were largest—among men without college education," they wrote. This finding suggests that as we move towards a more unequal society, we will end up imprisoning a larger and larger fraction of our population. Again, the biggest share of the burden will probably be borne by the wealthy, who will pay the bulk of the taxes needed to build new prisons.

Looking at the overall picture, academics have come to conflicting conclusions about the effects of inequality on economic growth. One of the most recent analyses, by Abhijit Banerjee and Esther Duflo of the Massachusetts Institute of Technology, suggests that *any* change in inequality—either an increase or a decrease—can lead to slower growth. But like their predecessors, the professors based their conclusion on data from many countries.

The United States could be different. It seems to have a unique tolerance for inequality, perhaps because of a high rate of income mobility. Americans are more likely to shoot up through the socioeconomic ranks—and fall down through them—than most other people. And yet they choose not to have the same sturdy safety net as most other wealthy nations do. Rather than paying higher taxes to ensure that any fall from grace would be cushioned, they prefer to focus on the climb upwards. Once again, they see only the upside risk—a classic case of overoptimism.*

In the coming years, the United States could easily become an exception to any broad-based rule about inequality's effects, for reasons ranging from its rags-to-riches ethos to the simple enormity of the changes being wrought by the neoconomists. But even if inequality does not become a problem for the economy, the incentives created by the neoconomy probably will.

Fast-forward to 2012 again. The neoconomists have had their way—all the taxes on saving and wealth have disappeared. And yes, Arnold Schwarzenegger is the 44th president.

So what's it like to be a citizen of the neoconomy? How would you make your most basic financial decisions? All your income from working would be taxed, and you'd be forced to save some of it in a financial portfolio to pay for your Social Security benefits. None of your income from other forms of saving would be

---

* This passage draws on some of my own unpublished research from my time as a graduate student. Using government surveys, I studied the relationship between people's tastes for redistribution (a safety net) and the volatility of income in the sorts of jobs they held. The people in occupations and industries with higher income volatility actually wanted less redistribution, all other things equal, signifying either overoptimism or enjoyment of risk. The latter explanation seemed less likely, since people are often risk-averse when it comes to the wages that pay for their necessities.

taxed, however. If you could choose where your income came from, you'd clearly have an incentive to shift more and more of it into the latter category.

After appraising the situation, you might decide to work a little less and spend more time managing your stock portfolio. Or, you might try to find ways for your employer to pay you in securities rather than in wages or salaries. Perhaps you'd buy special shares in your company that were only available to employees, and the shares would pay a dividend in lieu of a salary. You wouldn't be able to write a contract to guarantee those dividends, but millions of Americans have long been used to working without a contract. All the income you received as dividends would be tax free in the neoconomy, at least until the Internal Revenue Service caught on. Then you and your employer would have to find another loophole.

Tax lawyers, accountants and financial planners would be glad to help you find that loophole. You might have thought that their business would suffer in the neoconomy, with so many taxes gone—not so! With the help of these professionals, huge chunks of income would start shifting away from taxed sources and into untaxed sources.

As a result, the tax base would begin to shrink, if it hadn't done so already. At the same time, the government would be paying monthly benefits and medical costs for the nation's biggest-ever crop of retirees. These trends would not show any sign of reversing, so borrowing to deal with them wouldn't be possible. With a shrinking tax base and rising spending, there would be no alternative: tax rates would have to rise.

Who would be paying the higher rates? It would depend on who had the most success in shifting their income away from wages and salaries. In this race to avoid the grabbing hand of the Internal Revenue Service, the wealthiest people would obviously have had a head start. They were already receiving a lot of income from dividends, interest payments and the like, and they were also likely to be on first-name terms with at least one financial adviser.

The ones who would have the hardest time making the switch would be the working Americans who received most of their income from the sweat of their brow, or from the stain on the back of their swivel chair. For example, Wal-Mart might be renowned as a forward-looking company, but would it jump at the chance to pay its thousands of clerks with securities rather than cash? In any case, if you were a Wal-Mart clerk, you might not want to rely on a bond in place of a paycheck. For one thing, bonds usually pay interest on a quarterly or annual basis, rather than every week or every month. Say you just joined the company—how would you make ends meet until your first *quarterly* paycheck arrived?

People who work on fixed contracts, such as unionized auto workers, might also have a hard time grasping the brass ring of tax-free pay. Say you were working on an assembly line for General Motors, another one of the nation's biggest employers. According to your contract, you would receive fixed hourly pay and additional amounts for overtime; there would be other rules about annual raises, vacations, sick days and the like. In order to receive the same deal in a tax-free format, all those clauses would have to be written into the conditions of a bond or other financial asset. At that point, it might start looking too much like a labor contract for the Internal Revenue Service's taste.

Many low-income Americans would have a hard time saving, regardless of how they received their pay, so they wouldn't reap the full benefits of the neoconomy. Many of those who did save would have to pay off credit cards and second mortgages before they could buy income-producing assets. By the time these folks paid off their debts and started to save on a net basis, wealthier people would have been well on their way to entirely tax-free incomes, leaving the rest of working America to pay the taxes.

So how high would tax rates have to rise on the Americans who still worked? In 2001, about 18 percent of taxable income came from sources that would no longer be taxed in the neoconomy. If the government kept spending money at the same clip, tax rates would have to rise by about 18 percent, in some combination, just to make sure the federal deficit wasn't any bigger than it was in 2001. For example, if the rates went up evenly, the 10 percent bracket would become the 12 percent bracket, the 25 percent bracket would become the 29 percent bracket, and so on. And given that federal spending's share of the economy had already risen by about 11 percent in two years of the Bush administration's budgets, chances are that rates would have to rise even more.

The fortunate and growing minority who managed to receive all their income from stocks, bonds and other securities would pay nothing—not a dime—for America's cancer research, its international diplomacy, its military deterrent, the maintenance of the interstate highway system, the space program or almost anything else the federal government did. The only exceptions would be Social Security and Medicare, assuming they were still funded by the payroll tax—not necessarily the best assumption given the neoconomists' taste for a privatized system. Broadly speaking, that fortunate minority would be free-riders.

How long would working Americans stand for this sort of thing? Probably not very long. The situation would recall the feudalism many of the first Americans were trying to get away from when they left Europe. It would take only a few more steps to return to medieval times, when the landowning aristocracy levied taxes on the poor peasants to pay for their wars. If this lopsided economic situation came to pass, politicians would soon find themselves forced to make changes.

Yet reinstating abolished taxes wouldn't be easy. Only twice in the nation's history has a major federal tax been brought back from the dead. Both times, in 1894 and 1913, it was the personal income tax. Both times, moral and philosophical issues lay at the center of the debate. The second time even involved a constitutional amendment. At the very least, a permanent change in taxation requires 60 votes in the Senate.

One tax might not pose such a daunting task, however. Bringing back the estate tax wouldn't cause many problems in the economy. What's more, the people who would pay it might even welcome it.

According to research by David Joulfaian, an economist at the Treasury, the estate tax has had little effect on people's behavior. If anything, the tax has caused wealthy people to make more tax-exempt gifts to charity. And when George W. Bush proposed eliminating the estate tax, there was a surprising public outcry. More than 1,100 people who said they would be directly affected by the estate tax—ranging from actor Paul Newman to financier George Soros—signed their names to a "Call to Preserve the Estate Tax" issued in February 2001 by a lobbying group called Responsible Wealth. That petition argued for reforming the tax, perhaps by exempting estates worth up to $3.5 million without cutting the tax rate.

Warren E. Buffett, the investment guru who may briefly have become the world's wealthiest person in the fall of 2003, refused to sign.* He declined not because he wanted to abolish the estate tax, however, but because

---

* At the time of this writing, there was a reasonably energetic debate about whether Mr. Buffett, Bill Gates or Ingvar Kamprad, the founder of IKEA, was the world's wealthiest person. On October 26, 2003, the *Mail on Sunday* reported that Mr. Buffett overtook Mr. Gates, the Microsoft chairman, as the software maker's share price dropped. *Forbes* placed Mr. Gates top, ahead of Mr. Buffett, as of May 2004. There is some dispute about whether Mr. Kamprad still owns a substantial stake in IKEA.

he did not think the petition went far enough. In an interview with *The New York Times* (February 13, 2001), he actually echoed some of Professor Piketty's sentiments regarding inequality:

> Mr. Buffett said repealing the estate tax "would be a terrible mistake," the equivalent of "choosing the 2020 Olympic team by picking the eldest sons of the gold-medal winners in the 2000 Olympics." "We would regard that as absolute folly in terms of athletic competition," he said. "We have come closer to a true meritocracy than anywhere else around the world," he said. "You have mobility so people with talents can be put to the best use. Without the estate tax, you in effect will have an aristocracy of wealth, which means you pass down the ability to command the resources of the nation based on heredity rather than merit."

The estate tax was a relatively small target on the neoconomists' hit list, however, and reinstating it would only melt the tip of the iceberg of the neoconomy. Reinstating more taxes would not necessarily be easy, but politicians would also have other options for moving on from the neoconomy. A totally new tax, like a nationwide sales tax, might be more likely to emerge from Washington. But even that tax would exempt a huge portion of the wealthiest Americans' incomes; every year, they spend far less than they earn. Regardless of the solution, immense dislocations in the economy would be likely to result as Americans adapted to yet another set of rules.

It would all depend on how completely some Americans reacted to the new incentives the neoconomy created, and then on how violently other Americans reacted to those Americans' reactions. The vision of higher saving rates, a growing capital stock and accelerating innovation relied on Americans to be the sort of rational agents on whom economists based their models. Yet for the neoconomy, this rationality could become a double-edged sword.

In essence, the neoconomy could fail even if it succeeded. All the effort and resources devoted to it would amount to zilch—a complete waste.

EPILOGUE

The time to stop a revolution is at the beginning,
not the end.

—ADLAI STEVENSON

By now, this book should have convinced you that the pursuit of the neoconomy has opened up the nation to a vast new world of uncertainty. By changing the tax system and shifting the distribution of resources in the economy, the neoconomists might be pushing the nation to the brink of untold prosperity. They might also be dragging the economy on a wild goose chase, having passed up more promising ways of using the nation's wealth. But even if the economy gets close to achieving the neoconomists' vision, there is a danger that the final steps could result in chaos.

You've probably made up your own mind about the wisdom of the neoconomists' actions and future plans. But what motivated the neoconomists themselves? It's worth remembering that these men were all extremely smart and successful. They had already achieved great stature in their fields and a generous measure of material success. But George W. Bush had presented them with a once-in-a-lifetime opportunity: a chance to test their theories in the world's biggest economic laboratory.

That test—the neoconomists' revolution, imposed from above—was supposed to lead to a wealthier, more efficient economy. In this case, what was good for America would be good for the neoconomists, too. If we all got rich, the neoconomists would be heroes in academia and in Washington.

The neoconomists were not the ones actually making the big decisions about economic policy, however. They offered advice. Someone else had to make the judgments and pick the priorities, in what was always a political exercise. It seems fair to assume that this someone—putting aside rumors of others' ability to control him—was George W. Bush. And his incentives might not have been quite so well-aligned with those of the American people.

President Bush, like all politicians, probably had two goals in mind when forming his economic policies: helping the nation and getting re-elected. He declared his devotion to the first goal time after time, often giving speeches with backdrops emblazoned with slogans like "Strengthening America's Economy" or "Jobs Growth Opportunity." As in the neoconomists' case, achieving this first goal would have been good for George W. Bush as well as America; presidents, too, generally want to leave a positive historical legacy.

The second goal never made an appearance in the

president's public rhetoric, but its importance should not be underestimated. Virtually every president wants to be re-elected after his first term. And George W. Bush may have wanted four more years more than most presidents, given his father's one-term-and-out record.*

To figure out just how important a second term really was, an economist might try to see what the president revealed by his actions. His attempt at limiting steel imports with heavy tariffs—declared illegal by the World Trade Organization in November 2003—was almost certainly a play for votes in steel-producing states. Likewise, his refusal to be swayed by a Congressional consensus in favor of allowing travel to Cuba was probably intended to assuage his fervently anti-Castro supporters in Florida. Then there was the fulfillment of a central promise of his campaign: a prescription drug benefit as part of a revamped Medicare. Shortly after the promise became law, the White House predicted that the Medicare legislation, originally priced at $394 billion from 2004 to 2013, would actually cost $540 billion—a figure that dwarfed the tax cuts of 2003.

But President Bush's most revealing behavior, far and away, had to be the cross-country campaigning he began in May 2003: an all-out sprint that allowed him to amass a war chest of $159 million by the end of February 2004, according to his campaign's report to the Federal Election

* Readers may be thinking of Lyndon B. Johnson, who decided not to run for a second elected term. Whether he wanted to be re-elected, of course, is not the same as whether he thought he could win.

Commission. The fund was still growing rapidly at the time of this writing, even though the president did not have to spend any of that money on the Republican primaries, where he faced no competition.

If we accept, on the basis of this evidence, that President Bush cherished re-election, then we can begin to understand his constant urgency in pushing forward new tax cuts and other changes in economic policy. He had faced huge challenges. A recession began two months after he took office, and some earth-shaking shocks followed. Fear of a messy war in Iraq—for which the president himself bore much of the responsibility—paralyzed the economy for months. The labor market bled jobs throughout much of his term. Judging by precedent, it would have been difficult for him to win another term without putting the economy back on a track of strong growth.

So George W. Bush took the neoconomists' ideas and ran with them, as fast as he possibly could, grabbing resources from the present and future. What was a revolution in economic efficiency to the neoconomists might have seemed like a fight for survival to him.

He used up all the expected budget surpluses, and hundreds of billions in surpluses that might have been collected years after he left office. He put off the problem of dealing with Social Security, because the atmosphere didn't seem right for the solution he preferred. He called for tax-free savings accounts that would grab more billions from future administrations. He advocated tax cuts that would widen inequalities and potentially lead to social and economic problems in the decades to come. He tried to modernize the federal government's involvement in education—a campaign promise—but largely neglected initiatives to improve training and promote innovation.

Nevertheless, George W. Bush did give the economy a couple of shots in the arm, and he gave the nation a chance at faster growth in the future. Though he may have been predisposed to believe in the neoconomists' theories, he had a real interest in making sure that they worked in practice.

But if he wins re-election, will he follow through, and try to ensure that the neoconomy arrives?

It's hard to say. His motivation will have changed, since he won't be able to run for a third term. Presumably he won't work quite so hard on behalf of an unknown successor, even if that successor might be his brother or a very imposing former bodybuilder. The economy probably won't go through a similar run of shocks for many years. With little urgency and not much budgetary wiggle-room, George W. Bush might be tempted to leave the neoconomy hanging.

He won't necessarily have people to prod him along. The unanimity that characterized the early days of his administration has dissolved into a mix of different views. John W. Snow, the Treasury secretary, has been enthusiastically championing the neoconomists' proposals. But Stephen Friedman, the White House economic adviser who used to sit on the Concord Coalition's board, may be a skeptical budget hawk at heart. And an even greater divide might exist between Joshua Bolten, the director of the White House's Office of Management and Budget, and N. Gregory Mankiw, who took over from Professor Hubbard as chairman of the Council of Economic Advisers.

Just read what Mr. Bolten had to say, on July 15, 2003, even as he predicted a record deficit of $455 billion for that year: ". . . all economists, I think, will agree very strongly that when you reduce taxes, put more money back into the economy, that has a feedback effect in the economy that causes growth and in term increases receipts."

But only a few years earlier, Professor Mankiw, lately of Harvard University, had written the following in his best-selling textbook:

> People on fad diets put their health at risk but rarely achieve the permanent weight loss they desire. Similarly, when politicians rely on the advice of charlatans and cranks, they rarely get the desirable results they anticipate. After Reagan's election, Congress passed the cut in tax rates that Reagan advocated, but the tax cut did not cause tax revenue to rise. Instead, tax revenue fell, as most economists predicted it would, and the U.S. federal government began a long period of deficit spending, leading to the largest peacetime increase in the government debt in U.S. history.

Professor Mankiw wrote that there was "no credible evidence" suggesting people would work enough to offset the effect of lower tax rates on the government's revenue. In early 2004, there still wasn't. Furthermore, Mr. Bolten's comments didn't fit with the neoconomists' agenda. No matter how much more the nation saved, tax revenue could not possibly rise if the taxes on the return to saving were abolished. The revenue would have to come from other taxes, indirectly, over a period of years, if it came at all.

Professor Feldstein, the neoconomists' mentor, argued that the tax cuts would indeed cause people to work more. He urged politicians not to reverse any of the Bush administration's cuts, but he stopped short of recommending the further cuts that would have made the neoconomy a reality. Control of spending would ensure that the federal government's budget deficit shrank down to more manageable proportions within a few years, he wrote in *The Wall Street Journal* on February 12, 2004. He also noted, however, that sustained deficits of the size projected for 2004 would pose a very real threat to corporate investment—enough, one would think, to sabotage the neoconomy completely.

These crosswinds may well dampen President Bush's resolve, or they might lead him to slow down the pace of his economic revolution. Yet even if they do, some of the steps the neoconomists encouraged him to take will be difficult to reverse. Several of the tax cuts will expire in election years, giving politicians a chance to base their campaign platforms on extending the cuts. In 2004, the 10 percent tax bracket, increased child tax credit, depreciation bonuses for businesses will expire. So will the provisions offering tax relief to married couples filing jointly and middle-income filers subject to the alternative minimum tax. In 2008, the rates on dividends and capital gains will return to their original, higher levels.

Candidates for Congress and the White House will have a ready-made campaign slogan: "Vote for me, and I'll make sure these tax hikes never happen!" Going back to pre–2001 rates as specified in existing law is not exactly a hike, of course, but semantic arguments generally don't score points in political debates. George W. Bush knew this, and he didn't hesitate to use it in his own campaign. For example, here's what he said at a factory in Springfield, Missouri, on February 9, 2004: "There are some in Washington and they're going to say, let's not make the tax cuts permanent. That means it's going to raise your taxes. When you hear people say, we're not going to make this permanent, that means tax increase."

When Americans vote to elect a president, they will have a chance to make up their own minds. They may want to make all the tax cuts of George W. Bush's first term permanent, to institute those tax-free saving accounts, and to eliminate any remaining taxes on saving and wealth. Or they may decide that the neoconomy poses risks that are just too great for the budget, the economy and the capitalist system. There will always be disagreement about which choice is the right one, especially since economics offers no airtight answers or solutions. The voters will have to see through the rhetoric, then grasp the economic reality and make their choice.

SOURCES, NOTES AND EXPLANATIONS

Government Statistics

The federal government includes several units with exclusive responsibility for tracking different areas of the economy. The following is a list of the bureaus, agencies and departments, along with the types of statistics they keep. For brevity, the list only includes types of statistics that have been used in this book. All data were downloaded from the units' public websites. I have endeavored to use data adjusted for changes in prices and/or seasonal patterns wherever available and appropriate. Where the source of specific data might be ambiguous, I name the source in the endnotes.

Bureau of the Census (Commerce Department, www.census.gov):

Population estimates for recent years and current year; population projections for the next several decades; fraction of the population living in poverty by various measures; household and family measures of income

Bureau of Economic Analysis (Commerce Department, www.bea.gov):

Size and disposition of the national economy: spending by consumers, businesses and government; income broken down by type;

trade balances; rates of economic growth; corporate profits; saving rates; size and disposition of state economies

Bureau of Labor Statistics (Labor Department, www.bls.gov):

Unemployment and employment measured two ways: surveys of the population, and data on business and government payrolls; unemployment rates; labor force participation rates; workers' productivity; price indexes for goods and services purchased by households and businesses

Centers for Medicare & Medicaid Services (Health and Human Services Department, www.cms.hhs.gov):

Medicaid and CHIP enrollment figures and waiver information

Congressional Budget Office (Congress, www.cbo.gov):

Fiscal deficit/surplus projections; forecasts for economic growth; forecasts for the public debt; costs of legislation under consideration or passed by Congress (often with the Joint Committee on Taxation); monthly budget statistics (from data supplied by the Treasury)

Council of Economic Advisers (White House, www.whitehouse.gov/cea):

Economic Report of the President, which includes commentary and tables of historical data—notably on the federal budget—culled from several other agencies' reports, as well as a list of current and former members of the council.

Employment and Training Administration (Labor Department, www.doleta.gov):

Statistics on state unemployment insurance programs and federal supplements

Energy Information Administration (Energy Department, www.eia.doe.gov):

Prices for refined and unrefined fossil fuels: crude oil, natural gas, gasoline, etc.

Federal Reserve Board of Governors (www.federalreserve.gov):

Interest rates; levels of consumer and commercial debt; utilization of industrial capacity; speeches by Alan Greenspan and other officials

Internal Revenue Service (Treasury, www.irs.gov):

Income garnered and taxes paid by individuals, families and companies

National Center for Education Statistics (Education Department, nces.ed.gov):

Life expectancy calculations and estimates

National Center for Health Statistics (Centers for Disease Control, www.cdc.gov/nchs):

Life expectancy calculations and estimates

Social Security Administration (www.ssa.gov):

Historical documents; payroll tax rates over time; survival rates; worker-to-beneficiary ratios; balance sheets for the program from the Office of the Chief Actuary

THOMAS (Library of Congress, thomas.loc.gov):

Complete information on all bills introduced in Congress, including summaries written by the Congressional Research Service

Specific Items

I have cited several of my own articles here, on the advice of *The New York Times*, to protect myself from stealing my best ideas without attribution.

Introduction

2   "a third of the entire world's output . . . ": From a comparison of the World Bank's figures on the global economy in 2002 with the Bureau of Economic Analysis's figures for the United States in the same year (all in 2002 dollars).

2   "the nation's median annual income": Adjusted gross income reported in the Internal Revenue Service's Statistics of Income for tax year 2001.

2   cost of educating North Carolina's young people: The Census estimates that there were just under 1.5 million people aged 5 to 17 in North Carolina in 2002; according to the Bureau of the Census, the average cost of education per pupil in the nation's public schools was $7,284 in 2000–2001.

2   cost of a B–2 Spirit bomber: Taken from the U.S. Air Force

fact sheet (www.af.mil/factsheets/fs_82.shtml), 1998 dollars adjusted for inflation.

Chapter 1

8   "In 1999, the Clinton administration outlined a plan": See, for example: the Treasury website (www.ustreas.gov), press release LS-42, "Statement by Lawrence H. Summers, Secretary of the Treasury," August 4, 1999.

12 "the nation's median household income grew": In 2001 dollars the figures would be $39,869 and $43,162.

14 "research conducted in the 1980's and 1990's": Articles by Eugene Fama and Kenneth R. French, and James H. Stock and Mark W. Watson, are good places to start.

14 "The main index of the Nasdaq over-the-counter market": This calculation and others involving major market indices were made using free data from BigCharts.com.

16 "from Switzerland's UBS to San Francisco's Bank of America": UBS media release, "Swiss Economy Defies US Drop in Growth," January 19, 2001 and Bank of America, "U.S. Economic Projections Report," week of February 5, 2001; one could also contrast the changes in *The Economist*'s monthly poll of forecasters with the predictions in the Congressional Budget Office's January and May reports on the budgetary situation.

16 "'education recession' . . . ": Frank Bruni, "Giving Praise to Clinton, Bush Says Gore Is Flawed," *The New York Times,* September 29, 2000.

16 "Dick Cheney said": NBC News Transcripts, *Meet the Press,* December 3, 2000.

17 "George Bush echoed": CBS News Transcripts, *60 Minutes II,* December 6, 2000.

17 Edward F. McKelvey quote: Peter G. Gosselin, "A Bearish Bush Has Economists Worrying," *Los Angeles Times,* December 26, 2000.

18 "Money spent on imports": This calculation assumes that the government's spending on imports is negligible. For each year, I have divided imports (valued at current prices) by the sum of total private consumption, total private domestic investment and imports.

Chapter 2

21 "Even the ancient Romans": See, for example, Tacitus's *Annals of (Imperial) Rome: Book VI*, Tiberius seeds the banking system to forestall a credit crunch; Book XIII, during the consulship of Nero and Lucius Calpurnius Piso (V), sellers in the slave market raise prices in response to the lifting of a tax; Book XV, Nero fixes prices in the corn market despite a shortage, then fills the public coffers while criticizing his predecessors for lacking fiscal discipline.

27 "another generation of economists added a twist": For a brief history of this theory, called "endogenous growth," see Robert Barro and Xavier Sala-i-Martin, *Economic Growth* (McGraw-Hill, 1995); the text cites landmark papers by Paul M. Romer and others, as well as outlining the theory's predecessors.

Chapter 3

31 John F. Kennedy quote: From a compilation by the JFK Library at the University of Massachusetts, Boston (www.cs.umb.edu/jfklibrary).

32 "An economic adviser named Arthur B. Laffer": See, for example: Arthur B. Laffer, "Government Exactions and Revenue Deficiencies," *Cato Journal*, Spring 1981.

34 "shape up or ship out": David Hoffman, "Blames Tax Cuts, Defense Buildup; Feldstein Is Warned on Deficit Stance," *The Washington Post*, December 1, 1983.

34 "They finished their doctorates" (and future references to links between the Bush economic team and Martin S. Feldstein): David Leonhardt, "Scholarly Mentor to Bush's Team," *The New York Times*, December 1, 2002.

36 Hubbard excerpt: As of May 2004, the excerpt was on the American Enterprise Institute's website.

37 Hubbard quote: From a Federal Document Clearing House (FDCH) transcript of his testimony before the House Ways and Means Committee on April 15, 1997.

38 Martin S. Feldstein quotes: Martin S. Feldstein, "Fiscal Policies, Capital Formation and Capitalism," *European Economic Review*, Vol. 39, Nos. 3–4 (April 1995).

40 George W. Bush on *60 Minutes II:* CBS News Transcripts, *60 Minutes II*, December 6, 2000.

41 "the family's main hope": See, by way of indication: William Finnegan, "The Cuban Strategy," *The New Yorker,* March 15, 2004.

43 Center for Public Integrity study: Derrick Wetherell, "Snapshot of Professional and Economic Interests Reveals Close Ties Between Government, Business," *The Public i,* January 16, 2002.

43 summary of the wealth of the Bush administration: Thomas B. Edsall, "Bush Has a Cabinet Full of Wealth," *The Washington Post,* September 18, 2002.

45 the planning fallacy: Dan Lovallo and Daniel Kahneman, "Delusions of Success," *Harvard Business Review,* July 2003.

Chapter 4

56 "an extra year in a four-year college": See, for a summary: Orley Ashenfelter et al., "A Review of Estimates of the Schooling/Earnings Relationship, with Tests for Publication Bias," *Labour Economics,* Vol. 6, No. 4 (November 1999).

56 "Over his entire career": For this calculation, I assumed the man would work until age 65; there's no need to discount these figures by any more than the rate of inflation (already implied in the wage growth of 1 percent), since the federal government is infinitely patient.

57 "the College Board estimated": This comes second-hand, from the U.S. Chamber of Commerce's "College Savings Plan" financial calculator, online at www.uschamber.com; the 2001–2 figure appears to square with the College Board's current estimates, online at www.collegeboard.com.

58 "research has consistently found that on-the-job training is more effective": Daniel Altman, "Enhancing Education, Not Protecting Beleaguered Industries, Will Help the Economy, Experts Say," *The New York Times,* July 28, 2003.

58 "the Treasury forgoes less than $1 billion a year": From the Treasury website (www.ustreas.gov), press release RR–3234, "Treasury Deputy Assistant Secretary of Tax Analysis Leonard Burman: Testimony Before the House Ways and Means Subcommittee on Oversight," July 1, 1999.

62 "Bela Berenyi of Mercedes-Benz": Public Broadcasting System transcripts, *NOVA,* February 16, 1999.

63 Guglielmo Marconi quote: From the Nobel Foundation website (www.nobel.se), "Nobel Lecture, December 11, 1909: Wireless Telegraphic Communication."

63 "A report by CHI Research . . . ": Francis Narin, "Patents and Publicly Funded Research," in *Assessing the Value of Research in the Chemical Sciences* (National Academy Press, 1998).

65 "The Council of Economic Advisers summarized the results . . . ": Council of Economic Advisers, "Supporting Research and Development to Promote Economic Growth: The Federal Government's Role," October 1995.

65 "each dollar spent on research": These dollar figures represent the future payoffs from research in terms of their present value.

66 James D. Adams excerpt: James D. Adams, "Fundamental Stocks of Knowledge and Productivity Growth," *Journal of Political Economy,* Vol. 98, No. 4 (August 1990).

66 "A study published in 1998 . . . ": Austan Goolsbee, "Does Government R&D Policy Mainly Benefit Scientists and Engineers?" *American Economic Review,* Vol. 88, No. 2 (May 1998).

Chapter 5

77 "the biggest personal deduction of them all": Not counting the standard deduction or the one for dependents. The Joint Committee on Taxation estimated that the 32.1 million people who took advantage of that deduction, by counting the interest they paid on home loans against their taxable income, saved a total of $64.5 billion in taxes in 2001.

78 "three economists had released an exhaustive study of saving rates": Karen E. Dynan, Jonathan Skinner and Stephen P. Zeldes, "Do the Rich Save More?" *National Bureau of Economic Research Working Paper Series,* No. 7906 (September 2000); the income in question here is a sort of lifetime annual average.

80 "an estate had to be worth": Because the estate and gift taxes were combined, any large gifts made during the person's lifetime would subtract from the exempt amount.

81 "taxpayers would receive one-time checks": Each individual earning $6,000 or more and each married couple earning $12,000 or more would see their 2001 taxes fall by $300 and $600, respectively, under the new law. The checks merely meant that they would not have to wait until 2002 to feel the difference.

82 "A study by Matthew D. Shapiro and Joel Slemrod . . . ": Matthew D. Shapiro and Joel Slemrod, "Did the 2001 Tax Rebate Stimulate Spending? Evidence from Taxpayer Surveys," *National Bureau of Economic Research Working Paper Series,* No. 9308 (November 2002).

84 "The International Monetary Fund estimated . . . ": "United States 2001 Article IV Consultation, Staff Report," International Monetary Fund Staff Country Report No. 01/145 (August 2001).

84 "the figure could very easily stretch": This would occur if adjustments to the alternative minimum tax—a rule originally aimed at making sure the wealthy paid substantial taxes that was beginning to impose punitive rates on some middle class earners, too—were extended through 2010. Such extensions, or a similarly costly but more permanent fix, seemed likely to happen at the time of this writing.

85 Kent Conrad quote: From the Senate Budget Committee website (www.senate.gov/~budget/democratic), "Senate Budget Committee Chair Says New Economic Data Could Decrease Projected Budget Surplus."

85 Lawrence B. Lindsey quote: From the White House website (www.whitehouse.gov/news), "Remarks by Dr. Lawrence B. Lindsey at the Federal Reserve Bank of Philadelphia."

86 "new economic activity they were expected to generate in 2001 was $45 billion or less": Howard Gleckman, "The Tax Cut: Now You See It, Now You Don't," *BusinessWeek,* June 1, 2001.

88 "first major reform of the tax system in a generation": See, for example: from the White House website (www.whitehouse.gov/news), "Remarks by the President on Land and Water Conservation Fund," June 21, 2001.

90 "The latest academic research had shown that Head Start . . . ": See, for example: Eliana Garces, Duncan Thomas and Janet Currie, "Longer-Term Effects of Head Start," *American Economic Review,* Vol. 92, No. 4 (September 2002).

91 "the program's funding per student would actually have fallen": In the end, the changes were not instituted in 2001. But the House did approve, by one vote, a similar array of changes in July 2003. The Senate was yet to vote on a related bill at the time of this writing, though one had been introduced by Senator Judd Gregg, Republican of New Hampshire.

92 Greenwood quote: M. R. C. Greenwood, "Short Sight or Long View?" *University of California at Santa Cruz Currents,* March 26, 2001.

93 "they had shown themselves, in a government study, to be quite an effective stimulant for research": based on "The Effectiveness of Research and Experimentation Tax Credits," Office of Technology Assessment, U.S. Congress, September 1995.

94 George W. Bush quote: From the White House website (www.whitehouse.gov/news), "Remarks by the President in Tax Cut Bill Signing Ceremony," June 7, 2001.

Chapter 6

98 "230 million fewer passengers": Margie Mason, "Terror-wary Tourists Taking in the Woods and Fresh Air Instead of the Skies," Associated Press, October 17, 2001.

98 "the bottom dropped out of occupancy rates": Cecelia Blalock, "Industry Leaders Work with Government for Economic Recovery," *Hotel & Motel Management*, Vol. 216, No. 19 (November 5, 2001).

102 "Enron had also concealed billions in debts": See, for example: Daniel Altman, "Enron Had More Than One Way to Disguise Rapid Rise in Debt," *The New York Times*, February 17, 2002.

102 "It had disguised an amount": Compare the World Bank's data on Bolivia (available at www.worldbank.org) with the sum reported by the Senate Governmental Affairs Committee's Permanent Subcommittee on Investigations (from the FDCH transcript of its hearing on July 23, 2002); it's $8 billion in each case.

104 "the Standard & Poor's 500 index dropped": The index hit record highs of about 1,550 in March 2000 and stood at about 1,160 at the end of 2001—a drop of 25 percent. By late July 2002, the index had sunk to lows of about 780—an additional drop of 33 percent.

104 "the net effect could have been a wash": See, for a retrospective analysis: Daniel Altman, "Is Economic Double Dip Lurking on the Horizon?" *The New York Times*, July 29, 2002.

106 "as the Congressional Budget Office had predicted": From testimony of Dan L. Crippen, director of the Congressional Budget Office, before the Senate Budget Committee on September 4, 2001 (www.cbo.gov).

Chapter 7

110 George W. Bush quote from Appleton, Wisconsin: Dave Umhoefer, "Bush defends tax-cut proposal," *Milwaukee Journal Sentinel,* October 6, 2000.

111 George W. Bush quote from Chattanooga, Tennessee: From an FDCH e-Media transcript of the campaign appearance on November 6, 2000.

112 "a day that the Social Security trustees predicted would come": Board of Trustees of the Social Security Trust Funds, "The 2002 OASDI Trustees Report," updated January 29, 2003.

114 "investors and foreign central banks rushed to buy": See, for example: John M. Berry, "Treasury to Stop 30-Year Bond Sales; Surprise News Lifts the Securities' Price," *The Washington Post,* November 1, 2001.

116 "The discrepancy between short and long rates . . .": The analysis here comes from Daniel Altman, "History Isn't Quite Repeating on Rates," *The New York Times,* February 23, 2003. At the suggestion of Richard B. Berner, chief United States economist at Morgan Stanley, I later repeated the analysis, adjusting the interest rates for inflation. The discrepancy between the early 90's and the early 00's actually widened.

117 "Economists from academia and Wall Street debated the point": See, for example: Daniel Altman, "Rates Remain High. Blame Bush Budget or Big Expectations?" *The New York Times,* January 9, 2002.

118 Alan Greenspan quote: From the Federal Reserve Board of Governors website (www.federalreserve.gov), "Remarks by Chairman Alan Greenspan at the Bay Area Council Conference," January 11, 2002.

119 Paul H. O'Neill quote: From the Treasury website (www.ustreas.gov), press release PO-993, "Testimony of Treasury Secretary Paul O'Neill Before the Senate Budget Committee," February 7, 2002.

Chapter 8

123 George W. Bush quote: From an FDCH transcript, "George W. Bush Holds Media Availability," January 7, 2002.

125 "more than a dozen times": From the White House web site, press releases of February 27, March 1, March 27 (2), March

29, April 3, April 16, April 29, May 1, May 10, June 7, June 13 and June 14, 2002.

126 "and was expected to add $50 billion more": This estimate came from Robert A. Van Order, chief international economist at Freddie Mac, one of the big government-sponsored buyers of mortgages.

127 "whose principles President Bush had endorsed": From the White House website (www.whitehouse.gov/news), "President Unveils Back to Work Plan," October 4, 2001.

129 Bill Thomas quote: From the Ways and Means Committee website (waysandmeans.house.gov), "Opening Statement, Markup of H.R. 3090," October 12, 2001.

130 R. Glenn Hubbard quote: From an FDCH e-Media transcript of testimony before the Joint Economic Committee, May 23, 2001.

136 "After growing by 5 percent in the first quarter": At an annual rate, adjusted for inflation.

140 "A study headed up by Laurence H. Meyer . . . ": Laurence H. Meyer, "After an Attack on Iraq: The Economic Consequences," Center for Strategic and International Studies, November 21, 2002.

140 "many analysts judged it a disappointment": See, for example: Tracie Rozhon, "Margins Add Silver to a Cloudy Retailing Season," *The New York Times,* January 10, 2003.

141 *"The Economist* dubbed him 'tongue on the loose'. . . ": (No byline), "Tongue on the Loose: How Dangerous Is Paul O'Neill?" *The Economist,* June 28, 2001.

142 Paul H. O'Neill quote on tax policy: Richard W. Stevenson, "Bush Administration Says G.O.P. Tax Cut Bill Goes Too Far," *The New York Times,* October 16, 2001.

142 Paul H. O'Neill quote on Enron's collapse: H. Josef Hebert, "Cabinet Members Say They Didn't Inform Bush About Enron Calls for Help," Associated Press Business News, January 13, 2002.

143 "a war in Iraq might cost as much as $200 billion": Bob Davis, "Bush Economic Aide Says Cost of Iraq War May Top $100 Billion," *The Wall Street Journal,* September 16, 2002.

144 "was taken by surprise. . . ": See, for example: Mike Allen and Jonathan Weisman, "Bush Ousts O'Neill and Top Adviser," *The Washington Post,* December 7, 2002.

144 "He told the White House that he could extend the leave":

Edmund L. Andrews, "Bush Economic Adviser Says He's Not Finished Yet," *The New York Times*, January 24, 2003.

Chapter 9

151 "The productivity of the labor force": These figures are from the standard series quoted in the press and elsewhere. It represents the quarter-by-quarter change, at an annual rate, in the productivity of private sector employees who do not work on farms.

153 "raising deductibles and co-payments . . . ": Daniel Altman, "Inflation Is Alive in One Area of Medicine," *The New York Times*, January 26, 2003.

153 "A few held as much as 90 percent of their money in stocks": Daniel Altman, "The Economy May Be Facing More Hurdles," *The New York Times*, December 22, 2001.

154 "In the Wall Street Journal's semi-annual survey of economic seers . . . ": Table printed in *The Wall Street Journal*, January 2, 2003; available online from www.econstats.com.

157 "What the Bush administration stressed": Council of Economic Advisers, "Strengthening America's Economy: The President's Jobs and Growth Proposals," February 4, 2003.

163 "an estimate from the AFL-CIO": From the AFL-CIO website (www.aflcio.org): "Executive Paywatch Campaign Action Tools: Pension Funds, Mutual Funds and 401(k) Plans."

164 "There were other wrinkles": For a discussion of the dizzying details, see "Bush's Plan Taxes Certain Dividends, Fine Print Reveals," by Floyd Norris in *The New York Times*, January 9, 2003.

165 "the capital-related income that taxpayers declared": For capital-related income I'm using dividends, interest, net capital gains minus net losses, pension and annuity income, and net estate or trust gains minus net losses. I'm leaving out business and partnership income, since large portions of those might be more accurately equated with corporate profits or wages.

167 "This strategy had been tried before . . . ": Daniel Altman, "Deficit Spending Can Help Republicans," *The New York Times*, December 29, 2002.

170 David A. Wise quote: Daniel Altman, "Accounts Chock Full, or a Plan Half-Empty?" *The New York Times*, February 1, 2003.

171 Treasury press release and Pamela Olson quote: From the Treasury website (www.ustreas.gov), press release KD–3816, "President's Budget Proposes Bold Tax-Free Savings and Retirement Security Opportunities for All Americans," January 31, 2003.

173 "Rob Nichols, the top Treasury spokesman": Edmund L. Andrews, "Bush's Plan for Pensions Is Now Given Low Priority," *The New York Times,* February 26, 2003.

174 Allen Sinai quote: Daniel Altman, "Bush's Stimulus Plan and Its Two Big Ifs," *The New York Times,* February 18, 2003.

174 "real estate tycoons and the odd reporter": What follows is taken from my notes for a brief in *The New York Times* ("A Few Months in Washington and He's a Changed Man," February 23, 2003).

175 population of Medford, Oregon: From the City of Medford website (www.ci.medford.or.us), demographics section.

176 Norbert J. Ore quote: Daniel Altman, "Uncertain Economic Hinders Highly Precise Supply System," *The New York Times,* March 15, 2003.

179 Pamela Olson quotes: From the Treasury website, press releases JS–445 and JS–96, "Treasury Assistant Secretary for Tax Policy Pamela Olson Remarks to 2003 ICI/SIA Retirement Savings Conference," June 2, 2003 and "U.S. Assistant Treasury Secretary Pam Olson, Remarks to the Federal Bar Association 27th Annual Tax Conference," March 10, 2003.

179 John W. Snow quote: From the Treasury website, press release JS-999, "U.S. Treasury Secretary John W. Snow, Keynote Address to the Tax Foundation," November 13, 2003.

Chapter 10

181 "about 15 percent of all lifetime income": For this calculation, I assumed that such a retiree had worked for 40 years and would live to age 83 (the average life expectancy at age 65, according to the National Center for Health Statistics). According to the Social Security Administration, benefits for a middle-income worker replace about 40 percent of career earnings on an annual basis. The 18 years (from ages 65 to 83) at 40 percent of career earnings represent about 15 percent of total lifetime income.

188 "Academic studies have offered proof that Social Security

. . . ": The place to start in this literature is Martin S. Feld-stein, "The Effect of Social Security on Saving," *Contemporary Economic Analysis III* (Croon Helm: 1981).

194   "In a paper he authored in 1999 . . . ": Martin S. Feldstein, Elena Ranguelova and Andrew Samwick, "The Transition to Investment-Based Social Security When Portfolio Returns and Capital Profitability Are Uncertain," *National Bureau of Economic Research Working Paper Series,* No. 7016 (March 1999).

195   "an index of big companies' share prices that covers about 80 percent of the market": From an online description by Standard & Poor's (www.standardandpoors.com), down-loaded in November 2003.

197   "Newspapers reported that he would delay action . . . ": See, for example: Ron Hutcheson, "Bush Touts Social Security Plan," *The Philadelphia Inquirer,* March 1, 2002.

197   Joshua Bolten quote: (No byline), "Joshua Bolten and Dan Senor," *Christian Science Monitor,* October 9, 2003.

198   "the Bush administration deluged the media with leaks": See, for example: Donald Lambro, "Bush Intent on Revising Social Security; Re-Election Bid to Update Proposal," *The Washington Times,* November 20, 2003.

Chapter 11

203   "A study released in August 2002 by the Aspen Institute . . . ": David T. Ellwood et al., "Grow Faster Together. Or Grow Slowly Apart," Aspen Institute Domestic Strategy Group (www.aspeninstitute.org), August 2002.

204   Figures on education spending: From the Bureau of the Census website (www.census.gov), "Public Education Finances 2001," March 2003.

204   "The neoconomists' tax cuts and related initiatives": To make this rough calculation, I divided the Congressional Budget Office's estimated 11-year cost of the 2001 fiscal package ("Economic Growth and Tax Relief Reconciliation Act"), as passed, by 11 to get their average annual cost: $1.35 trillion over 11 years, or $123 billion a year on average. I then added the analogous figure for the 2003 fiscal package ("Jobs and Growth Tax Relief Reconciliation Act"): $350 billion over 11 years, or $31 billion a year. I did not add the interest costs, since they would be the same whether the government spent money or gave up tax revenue. I also rounded down the fractions of billions.

205 "For around $50 billion a year": This calculation uses the $26,000 figure from the College Board for the cost of a year at a private, four-year institution in 2001–2 (see Chapter 4), and the Education Department's count of 1.6 million first-year students at all colleges in the fall of 2001. Both figures could be expected to grow with time.

206 Budgets for basic research: Ronald L. Meeks, "President's Budget Includes Modest Increase for R&D in FY 2004; R&D Funding for Homeland Security Contributes to Defense, Science, Transportation, and Agriculture," InfoBrief NSF 04–300, National Science Foundation, October 2003.

208 Trade deficit as percentage of economy: Here the numerator is the December measurement of the trade deficit, and the denominator is the fourth-quarter reading of annualized gross domestic product divided by 12 (for 12 months).

209 "incomes less than half of the poverty line": This calculation is based on the federal poverty line for a family of four in 2002, which was income of $18,100 for the year.

209 Figures on hunger: Emily Gersema, "The Number of Hungry Families Is Increasing," Associated Press Worldstream, October 31, 2003 (based on a report by the U.S. Department of Agriculture).

211 "a lot of people who receive the benefits don't get new jobs": See, for example: Lawrence F. Katz and Bruce D. Meyer, "The Impact of Potential Duration of Unemployment Benefits on the Duration of Unemployment," *Journal of Public Economics*, Vol. 41, No. 1 (February 1990).

213 "Experts in Washington estimated": These figures come from some of my unused notes for an article in *The New York Times*.

213 "900,000 full-time workers lost their coverage": Ceci Connolly, "Census Finds Many More Lack Health Insurance," *The Washington Post*, September 30, 2003.

213 average HMO premiums: Aventis Pharmaceuticals, "HMO-PPO/Medicare-Medicaid Digest for 2002," *Aventis Managed Care Digest Series* (2003, based on data from SMG Marketing-Verispan LLC).

215 State budget deficits and cuts: National Association of State

Budget Officers, "The Fiscal Survey of the States" (May 2002, November 2002, June 2003).

Chapter 12

223 "the model *assumed* it": Daniel Altman, "Opinions on Economy Are Easy; Proof Is Tough," *The New York Times*, July 19, 2003.

228 "In the Federal Reserve's Survey of Consumer Finances . . . ": calculations using data compiled in Employee Benefit Research Institute, "Family Savings: Results of the Survey of Consumer Finances," April 2003.

230 Richard H. Clarida quotes: Daniel Altman, "Bush's Stimulus Plan and Its Two Big Ifs," *The New York Times*, February 18, 2003.

232 "A stunning coincidence": Namely: Paul Krugman, "Promises, Promises," *The New York Times* and Robert Barro, "Go Figure," *The Wall Street Journal*, both on March 9, 2004.

Chapter 13

236 "after-tax income different groups of taxpayers would control": The data on which these charts are based comes from a computer model maintained by Robert S. McIntyre, director of Citizens for Tax Justice, a lobby group.

241 Thomas Piketty quote: Daniel Altman, "Efficiency and Equity (In the Same Breath)," *The New York Times*, April 20, 2003.

243 "a team at Princeton University": Bruce Western, Meredith Kleykamp and Jake Rosenfeld, "Crime, Punishment, and American Inequality," Princeton University mimeo, June 2003.

243 "One of the most recent analyses . . . ": Abhijit V. Banerjee and Esther Duflo, "Inequality and Growth: What Can the Data Say?" *Journal of Economic Growth*, Vol. 8, No. 3 (September 2003).

247 "sources that would no longer be taxed": Here I'm including dividends, interest, capital gains and other forms of income derived from them: capital gains distributions, estate and trust income, and taxable pensions, annuities and Individual Retirement Accounts. I'm not including corporate profits or business income directly received by individuals, though a pure neoconomy probably wouldn't tax these, either.

247 "federal spending's share of the economy had already risen": The last year of federal spending primarily determined by a Clinton administration budget was 2001. Between the end of 2001 and the end of 2003 (the last quarter for which figures were available at this writing), federal spending rose to 6.9 percent of the economy from 6.2 percent, a rise of 11 percent in its share. Federal spending does not include entitlements like Social Security or veteran's benefits.

249 "According to research by David Joulfaian . . . ": This academic debate is summarized in Daniel Altman, "Does It Cost the Wealthy Too Much to Die?" *The New York Times,* June 30, 2002.

250 Warren E. Buffett quote: David Cay Johnston, "Dozens of Rich Americans Join in Fight to Retain the Estate Tax," *The New York Times,* February 14, 2001.

Epilogue

257 Joshua Bolten quote: From an FDCH e-Media transcript of the press briefing in Washington, D.C. on July 15, 2003.

257 N. Gregory Mankiw excerpt: From the second chapter of *Principles of Economics,* first edition (The Dryden Press: 1998).

257 "Control of spending would ensure": Martin S. Feldstein, "Here Are the Facts," *The Wall Street Journal,* February 12, 2004.

259 George W. Bush quote: From the White House website, press release: "President Meets with Workers and Small Business Owners on Economy," February 9, 2004.

INDEX

PublicAffairs is a publishing house founded in 1997. It is a tribute to the standards, values, and flair of three persons who have served as mentors to countless reporters, writers, editors, and book people of all kinds, including me.

I. F. STONE, proprietor of *I. F. Stone's Weekly*, combined a commitment to the First Amendment with entrepreneurial zeal and reporting skill and became one of the great independent journalists in American history. At the age of eighty, Izzy published *The Trial of Socrates*, which was a national bestseller. He wrote the book after he taught himself ancient Greek.

BENJAMIN C. BRADLEE was for nearly thirty years the charismatic editorial leader of *The Washington Post*. It was Ben who gave the *Post* the range and courage to pursue such historic issues as Watergate. He supported his reporters with a tenacity that made them fearless and it is no accident that so many became authors of influential, best-selling books.

ROBERT L. BERNSTEIN, the chief executive of Random House for more than a quarter century, guided one of the nation's premier publishing houses. Bob was personally responsible for many books of political dissent and argument that challenged tyranny around the globe. He is also the founder and longtime chair of Human Rights Watch, one of the most respected human rights organizations in the world.

For fifty years, the banner of Public Affairs Press was carried by its owner, Morris B. Schnapper, who published Gandhi, Nasser, Toynbee, Truman, and about 1,500 other authors. In 1983, Schnapper was described by *The Washington Post* as "a redoubtable gadfly." His legacy will endure in the books to come.

Peter Osnos, *Publisher*